Service, Prosperity And Sanity

Positioning the Professional Service Firm for the Future

By
Earl Maxwell

Maxwell Locke & Ritter, p.c.
100 Congress, Suite 1740
Austin, Texas 78701
Tel: (512) 474-5753 Fax: (512) 476-4386
http:www.mlrpc.com

Ordering Information

Individual Sales. Order directly from Maxwell Locke & Ritter.

Quantity Sales. Special discounts are available on quantity purchases by corporations, associations and others. For details, contact Maxwell Locke & Ritter at the address above.

Orders for college textbook/course adoption use. Please contact Maxwell Locke & Ritter at the address above.

Orders by U.S. trade bookstores and wholesalers. Please contact Maxwell Locke & Ritter at the above address.

Printed in the United States of America.
ISBN 0-9666011-0-6

Service, Prosperity and Sanity

Positioning the Professional Service Firm for the Future

Table of Contents

Preface--- The Journey

♦ The definition of insanity ♦ You don't have to reinvent the wheel. ♦ Why this book?
♦ External forces ♦ What this book does not do ♦ What this book is intended to do

---

"Insanity is doing the same thing over and over again and expecting a different result."

One of my partners referred to this well-known quotation during a strategic planning session in early 1993 as we focused on our CPA firm's financial results since its inception in early 1991. The discussion that ensued had a profound impact on our firm, and fundamentally changed our business culture and operating systems.

Often we are asked by people who hear about our firm's business culture, "what other firm operates in such a manner?"

Actually, when we embarked on our journey, we could not find a case study involving a professional service firm that had fundamentally changed its business culture to really position itself for the future. We could not find a firm that had seriously redefined its culture to incorporate progressive concepts implemented by many manufacturing, retail and distribution companies. There were some isolated examples of professional service firms implementing certain concepts, but we found no firm attempting the systemic change that we believed necessary. Most reengineering efforts of professional service firms focused on converting the culture from one in which managers and partners took orders and relied on referrals, to a role in which they aggressively marketed their services.

No one seemed serious about turning the traditional model upside down and implementing the systemic changes which were necessary.

You don't have to reinvent the wheel.

Professional service firms face a future filled with exploding technology, too little time and too much information. It's dangerous out there. The wrong moves can spell the death of your business enterprise. And the cost of doing nothing--well, nobody can afford that. In this book, we chronicle our journey and share our story of how we learned principles and techniques which can allow your business not only to survive the future, but *flourish.* We learned to:

- Trust your people.
- Support your families.
- Get involved in the community.
- Exercise courage.
- Move into uncomfortable zones.
- Share information openly.
- Use teams effectively.
- Know your Aim.
- Have fun.

We encourage you to tap into our firm's experience, strength and hope on critical issues such as the changing nature of financial services, the emerging workforce, open book management, profit sharing methodologies that really work, and most important, the development of values in your workplace that change the lives of you and your associates. Preparing a professional service firm for the future actually means transforming your business from top to bottom. It requires unwavering commitment to new, and at times revolutionary, ideas. Our story can help you learn new ways to look at commitment and achieve momentum--to successfully move you into the future--without *reinventing the wheel.*

Why this book?

This book is the story of how a small group of people radically changed the traditional model of a professional service firm in order to position themselves for the future. It explains how our firm chose not to participate in the declining profit trends of the public accounting profession. Although this book is not a "how-to" self-help practice management book, it is full of concepts and ideas that you can adapt to your firm's unique situation. Finally, this book provides a benchmark from which to begin an internal process of change to allow the professional service firm to take advantage, rather than become victims, of external forces such as:

- **Increased Consumer Demand**
- **Heightened Work Force Expectation**
- **Changing Demographics**
- **Technological Advances**

What this book does not do.

It is not the purpose of this book to convince anyone of the need for redefining the organizational structure of the professional service firm. This book does not devote much space to the history that led to the rapid rate of change we are experiencing, nor to the changes that are ahead of us. *I believe we have only seen the tip of the iceberg when it comes to the changes that are ahead.* This book does not provide the technical guidance that supports reengineering concepts. In this respect, it does not focus on the academics of management philosophies or organizational behavior. Instead, it refers to some of the books and reference materials which people in our firm read as we became convinced that unless we changed the model of our firm, we would be out of business in five years.

What this book is intended to do.

This book is for professional service firm leaders who are already absolutely convinced of the changing environment, and of the impact those changes will have on their business. Prospective readers are already struggling with how to go about redefining their own professional service firm. The purpose of this book is to help firm leaders deal with questions such as:

- **How do I convince my partners (especially the older ones) of the need to change?**
- **How will our people react to these changes?**
- **What will our clients think?**
- **How many of our people are capable of making these changes?**
- **How long will it take?**
- **How soon can we begin to see positive results?**
- **What can we expect to go wrong?**
- **What kind of help will we need?**
- **How do we begin?**

This book provides a practical guide to reengineering the professional service firm. If you are not in a leadership role but have access to a leader, you may want to read this book.

I hope you enjoy the Journey!!!

-- Earl Maxwell

Dr. W. Edwards Deming

Throughout this book, I refer to Dr. W. Edwards Deming as someone who had a profound effect in shaping our firm's thinking. He is considered by many to have been the primary leader of the sweeping quality revolution that improved the competitive position of the United States during the eighties. He is best known for his work in Japan where from 1950 and onward he taught top management and engineers quality concepts. This teaching dramatically altered the economy of Japan. Since the eighties, he provided the same knowledge to U.S. managers through his writings and seminars. The fourteen points which he considered as the basis for transforming American industry are condensed as follows:

1. Create constancy of purpose toward improvement of product and service, with the aim to become competitive and to stay in business, and to provide jobs.

2. Adopt the new philosophy. We are in a new economic age. Western management must awaken to the challenge, must learn the responsibilities, and take on leadership for change.

3. Cease dependence on inspection to achieve quality. Eliminate the need for inspection on a mass basis by building quality into the product in the first place.

4. End the practice of awarding business on the basis of price tag. Instead, minimize total cost. Move toward a single supplier of any one item, on a long-term relationship of loyalty and trust.

5. Improve constantly and forever the system of production and service, to improve quality and productivity, and thus constantly decrease costs.

6. Institute training on the job.

7. Institute leadership. The aim of the supervision should be to help people and machines and gadgets to do a better job. Supervision of management is in need of overhaul, as well as supervision of production workers.

8. Drive out fear, so that everyone may work effectively for the company.

9. Break down barriers between departments. People in research, design, sales and production must work as a team, to foresee problems of production and in uses that may be encountered with the product or service.

10. Eliminate slogans, exhortations, and targets for the work force asking for zero defects and new levels of productivity. Such exhortations only create adversarial relationships, as the bulk of causes of low quality and low productivity belong to the system and thus lie beyond the power of the work force.

11 a. Eliminate work standards (quotas) on the factory floor. Substitute leadership.

11 b. Eliminate management by objective. Eliminate management by numbers, numerical goals. Substitute leadership.

12 a. Remove barriers that rob the hourly worker of his right to pride of workmanship. The responsibility of supervisors must be changed from sheer numbers to quality.

12 b. Remove barriers that rob people in management and in engineering of their right to pride of workmanship. This means, inter alia, abolishment of the annual or merit rating and of management by objective.

13. Institute a vigorous program of education and self-improvement.

14. Put everybody in the company to work to accomplish the transformation. The transformation is everybody's job.

The fourteen points clearly provided our firm with the foundation upon which to begin and sustain our transformation.

Chapter 1. The Journey Begins-- How We Became Convinced

♦ A new kind of environment ♦ Philosophical statement ♦ Service, Prosperity and Sanity ♦ Values, creativity and innovation ♦ Comfort zones can be a barrier to change ♦ How our firm became convinced of the need to change ♦ Some not-so-positive observations about my earlier experience ♦ A harrowing realization about great resumes ♦ The system was also driven by fear ♦ How we went to the next level ♦ Writings which influenced my thinking ♦ My chance finally came during a visit to the home office ♦ Little did I know of the difficulties ahead

---

In 1993, Austin's economy was beginning to recover from a serious local depression that had begun in 1987. The good news was our firm, Maxwell Locke & Ritter, p.c. (ML&R), was well positioned in the marketplace, service delivery was sound and revenues were growing. The bad news was we were in a vicious cycle of working harder and making less money. The by-products of this cycle were obvious and cut to the core of our inability to make significant progress toward the overall goals of the firm.

Our people were tired and uninspired by the firm's and the profession's long-term prospects. Most of management's discussions revolved around the question of how to motivate our people to work as hard as we did.

How could we get our people to treat decisions and actions as if they owned the firm?

How could we keep pace with rapid changes around us?

In my role as managing shareholder of the firm, I was exhausted. I was tired of the idea that my job was to come in each day to make decisions for a bunch of people who, I eventually realized, were capable of making the decisions themselves. Also, I was tired of the patriarchal role of "taking care of people" and counseling them on what they needed to do to be more successful.

For fourteen years, I had been on the "fast track" of an international accounting firm. I had been in management positions for several of these years and the managing shareholder of our local firm for two years. Quite frankly, I found the traditional manager's role exhausting, particularly in light of the expectation that it was my job to make the decisions. And I mean *all* decisions.

What else should I have expected? This is what managers did.

I wanted to have my hand in everything so I could control projects, revenues, expenses and even people. I truly believed no one could do most of this as well as I could.

In fact, I spent a lot of time frustrated by my associates' seeming inability or lack of desire to work as hard as I did and get things right. Unmade decisions stacked up on my desk faster than I could make them. Even worse, I made most decisions in haste, when someone finally would come into my office and suggest digging into the stack until we found theirs. Other decisions were made slowly or not at all. Often, these unmade decisions had taken months to work their way up the organizational pyramid before they entered my stack.

Another aspect of the traditional public accounting environment is that it seemed to encourage complaining and negative attitudes. Over the years I became a part of this without really realizing it. People not only spent time complaining, they spent an inordinate amount of time participating in the "grapevine," one of the most effective means of communication in any office. Everyone kept an ear to the ground in order to hear the latest rumor, and some people enjoyed this aspect of the culture so much that on slow days they created new ones. Many phone conversations began with the question, "Heard any rumors today?" My frustration, coupled with the negative atmosphere in our office, led me to seek a change.

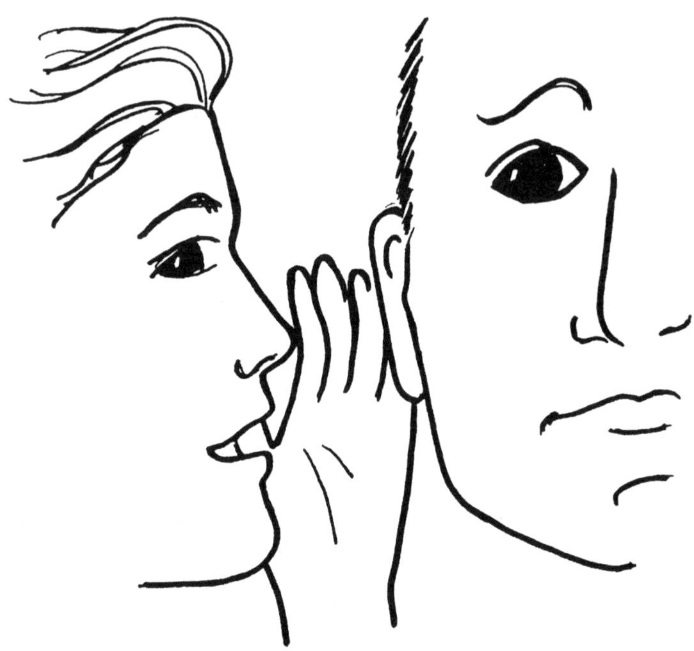

A new kind of environment.

In 1991, we began to establish a new kind of environment for an accounting firm, built on a foundation of people dedicated to:

- **Creating an environment where people do things because they want to, not because they are afraid not to.**
- **Encouraging open communication.**
- **Committing themselves and living up to their commitments.**
- **Treating everyone with honesty, dignity and respect.**
- **Serving our clients with the highest degree of competency, compassion and courtesy.**
- **Actively participating in the community.**
- **Treating others as we would like to be treated.**

We developed a philosophical statement that worked for us.

Provide highest quality solutions and services that our clients value from an environment which promotes each person's personal goals, self esteem and professionalism.

When we began ML&R, we believed it was important to create an environment that attracted and retained the best professionals. We believed any professional service firm that effectively accomplished this would also have the ability to attract and retain the best client base, to produce the best profits and provide the best salaries for our people. We saw a decent working environment as the beginning of a circular pattern leading to long term ***service, prosperity and sanity.***

In other words, we believe happy people make clients happy and happy clients pay their bills and want more of our service. We knew we could not satisfy all of our people. However, we were certain we could foster an environment that would provide a nice place to work and would enable those who shared the values of the firm to be happy and successful.

Every professional service firm says it supports this kind of environment, but few actually make the necessary changes to foster such an environment. Many firms demand that their people treat clients with care and compassion, but these same firms abuse their own people. Not surprisingly, this creates confusion.

We wanted to treat our people with dignity and respect. Our goal was to establish a foundation from which we never lost sight of the importance of serving our clients with the same dignity and respect.

Values, creativity and innovation.

Certain values became of paramount importance to us.

We believed the definition of prosperity could be more than simply a material focus on money. We also believed this new environment could bring better balance to our lives and restore sanity to the workplace.

Integrity and honesty were expected and demanded in our newly established firm. The greed and excesses of the eighties had significantly impacted how businesses and their leadership were perceived. As a result, many children believed the only way to get ahead in business was to lie, cheat and steal. How could we blame them? For a decade or more, most business news coverage focused on corporate raiders, insider trading, junk bonds, kickbacks, waste, fraud and abuse. We were determined to establish core values in our firm with the commitment to never compromise them. We believed our individual and firm reputations would become the hallmark of our organization.

Our traditional firm culture could not begin to keep pace with the rapid changes driven by technological advances, increased client demands, heightened work force expectations and shifting demographics. We believed these changes to be as significant as those of the Renaissance and the Industrial Revolution. If our premise was correct, innovation and creativity would become important factors in enabling us to meet the future needs of our clients. We knew the traditional organizational culture of the professional service firm did very little to support either creativity or innovation. Instead, it stifled creativity and aborted innovation. Regrettably, we knew our firm's culture was steeped in this traditional model.

Following a dynamic and, to many, frightening presentation by a knowledgeable futurist, fifty leading partners of America's most progressive CPA firms were asked to raise their hands if they were convinced of the radical changes that had just been presented. Most of the people in the audience raised their hands.

"How many of you have been converted?" queried the speaker.

Most of the audience seemed confused by the question.

"Being converted means you are in the process of implementing fundamental changes to your firm which will enable you to survive the future radical changes you are convinced will occur," said the speaker.

After a few uncomfortable moments, three or four hands rose. A long silence followed, after which the speaker suggested the audience and the profession should seriously consider its lack of response to something we were convinced would ultimately occur. The speaker then quietly stepped down to more silence, followed by the welcome relief of a coffee break.

Comfort zones can be a barrier to necessary change.

Why haven't more professional service firms converted?

Why aren't more organizations implementing fundamental changes to clearly position themselves for a more prosperous future?

My theory follows:

(1) Most professional service firms continue to be profitable and their owners continue to lead the comfortable lifestyles they have grown to expect. Therefore, a sense of urgency does not exist and the organization continues in its comfort zone. The "entitlement" attitude of management continues.

(2) Most firms are managed and controlled by people who are fifty or older. Some of these people do not really believe in the changes to come, while many do not believe the changes will occur before their watches end, or at least they hope not! In other words, they hope to retire before it becomes necessary for some of the younger partners to implement the difficult changes.

(3) Finally, most service providers who understand the need for change cannot be catalysts for redesigning the organizational model

because they either do not have a vote, or do not control a majority of the votes.

How did our firm become convinced?

As the managing shareholder of the newly formed ML&R, I probably started the process. The roots of becoming convinced date to the idealism of my teenage years, which happen to coincide with the counterculture period of the late sixties and early seventies. Upon graduation from college in 1976, I got a hair cut and accepted a position with one of the Big Eight accounting firms, which later became one of the Big Six. I followed the traditional career path of an auditor and in 1987 became a partner in the firm. During my fourteen years with the international accounting firm, I learned a great deal and met and interacted with many interesting and even a few brilliant people. I saw most of the United States and Latin America and ate in many of the world's finest restaurants. I had a wonderful time.

The experience also introduced me to the tremendous benefits of civic activities and the rewards of returning something to the communities that had been so good to me. It enabled me to become a decent accountant and a well-rounded business leader. Also, I developed the ability to analyze a variety of situations, balance a variety of forces in an organized way and present ideas in a convincing manner. And finally, I overcame a fear of public speaking that I had battled for many years.

Some not-so-positive observations about my earlier experience.

The culture of the Big Six accounting firm was steeped in the traditional corporate model of the post-World War II years. Over the years the firm became very successful and grew to over fifty thousand people.

Along with this success, a huge bureaucratic structure grew with the many hierarchies of the traditional pyramid. Over time the pyramid grew into four relatively independent pyramids--audit, tax, consulting and administration. Some people view these pyramids as silos or control towers. Whatever the view, the power of the organization rested at the top, where information was closely guarded by those who were entitled to it by virtue of years of dedicated service, huge personal sacrifice, and other rites of passage.

In this culture, information regarding the financial performance and strategies of the firm were closely guarded *secrets*. Partners often met behind closed doors. Everyone else in the firm wasted much time speculating about what was decided in those meetings and how the decisions would affect *them*. Often, people wondered who the next victims would be. As mentioned earlier, the most effective communication was gathered through the grapevine or through questioning secretaries, who typed or sorted confidential correspondence. Even worse, once a year the partners went to a national meeting to determine what the national office was going to do to them the next year. The partners received marching orders and information about how they should communicate the firm's strategies to the troops back home.

A harrowing realization about great resumes.

The system was driven by the assumption that younger professionals who were technically capable would work hard, go anywhere, and do anything required to ultimately achieve the money and security offered to partners. Sometimes this carrot worked for the ten to fourteen years required to become a partner. Some people waited even longer. Amazingly, this method worked for decades, even though only a very small percentage of the people who went to work for a Big

Six firm would eventually become partners. Everyone else generated as much revenue as possible for the benefit of the owners of the firm--and generate revenue we did. In 1981, I worked three months without a day off. In 1982, my first son was born in January and I hardly saw him awake until April. The other years were not really much different. Everyone accepted this work ethic, at least as long as they were employed, and some worked much more than I did. My observation over the years was that most people who worked excessively long hours burned out before their time and left the firm. In return, we learned a great deal and Big Six experience enhanced our resumes.

The system was also driven by fear.

I remember sitting in an orientation session with several hundred new hires being greeted by the managing partner of the firm. He asked us to look to our right and then to look to our left. He assured us that two of the three people involved in the motivational exercise would not be present for the new seniors' meeting in three years. He went on to say that only one in five of us would be present for the new managers' meeting in five or six years.

This really fired people up. The next day, one of the participants disappeared. A story spread among the rest of us that, apparently, the new hire had made a joke about the managing partner's heritage during the previous evening's reception. As a result, his career ended and he returned home to find another job. Fact or legend? Who knows?

On my first audit, the senior accountant told me my most important job was to take care of him and that any embarrassment I caused him would be the last. I never caused him any and I went on to the next level.

Now, these techniques seem absurd. However, they were effective at the time and clearly set the tone for the next fourteen years of my career. Employees' opinions were not important, and employees were afraid to express opinions for fear of offending someone higher on the corporate ladder. Fear drove many decisions--fear of not living up to someone's expectations, fear of looking bad, fear of going over budget on an audit or tax return, fear of offending a client, fear of not being promoted, fear of the consequences of not accepting a transfer to another office, and the ultimate fear of being fired or "counseled out." All of these situations were career limiting moves, referred to by staff as "CLMs." Certain situations were career ending moves or "CEMs." Accountants will develop an acronym for any occasion.

I did not fully comprehend the degree to which fear shaped situations until I had been away from the culture for some time. In fact, I did not comprehend much of what was happening until I left. Fourteen years of fear on the fast track did not permit much time for personal reflection.

Enough of the history and back to the question of how we became convinced. My history, together with becoming a student of "Total Quality Management" during the late eighties, led me to examine the traditional organizational structure of the professional service firm. I read books and magazines, listened to audio tapes, and attended TQM conferences.

Some of the writings that shaped my thinking are:
Out of the Crisis by W. Edwards Deming
The New Economics by W. Edwards Deming
In Search of Excellence by Tom Peters
Thriving on Chaos by Tom Peters
See You at the Top by Zig Ziglar
The Fifth Dimension by Peter Senge
Flight of the Buffalo by Ralph Stayer
Managing the Future by Peter F. Drucker
Managing in a Time of Great Change by Peter F. Drucker

Iacocca by Lee Iacocca
Talking Straight by Lee Iacocca
The Precious Present by Spencer Johnson
Money and the Meaning of Life by Jacob Needleman
The Seven Habits of Highly Successful People by Steven Covey
Built to Last by James C. Collins & Jerry L. Porras
The Wisdom of Teams by Jon R. Katzenbach & Douglas K. Smith
Competing for the Future by Gary Hamel & C. K. Prahalad
The Goal by Eliyahu M. Goldratt
The Employee Handbook of New Work Habits for a Radically Changing World by Price Pritchett

In addition, each month for six years I listened to two audio-taped business books produced by Fastrack. Many of these tapes dealt with topics discussed in this book.

As I began to translate TQM concepts from a ***manufacturing*** environment to a ***service*** environment, my excitement grew.

However, the reality of my situation tempered it. I was a line partner in a firm that had recently doubled its size by merging with another giant. The newly combined firm was immobilized by the corporate paralysis that immediately followed the "merger of two equals." This was worse because our office was an unprofitable second tier office, which was dying on the vine in a city mired in recession. There was no end in sight to the region's economic woes.

I felt like a U.S. soldier in the 1880s with a small troop stationed in a far west outpost. Obviously, this was not exactly a good test site for many of my ideas. The few we attempted were quickly undone by unrelated decisions made up the corporate ladder.

My chance finally came during a visit to the home office.

I suggested I would consider buying the accounting practice of our local office if the national firm had a similar interest. Within two weeks, we had a willing seller and a willing purchaser at the bargaining table. What I believed would be a simple task of determining the purchase price took six extremely difficult months of my life. The seemingly worthless local practice became very valuable to the national firm upon locating a willing buyer. Finally, we reached an agreement. Then, on a Saturday morning in February 1991, I opened the doors to an empty office and thrust both hands into the air as if I had won an Olympic Gold Medal. Now I had my opportunity to begin redefining the nature of public accounting--at least in our office. I no longer had the convenient excuses to absolve me of the inability to get done what I knew needed to be done. No longer could I blame the previous bureaucracy that had stifled attempts to challenge the establishment.

Little did I know of the difficulties ahead...

Chapter 2. How We Moved Toward Conversion

◆ Some subtle changes ◆ Early decisions more symbolic than substantive ◆ Forming the new ML&R in 1991 was not just turning the clock back to 1986 ◆ Herb Kelleher, an early mentor from the TQM movement, was twenty years ahead of most of the corporate world ◆ An early turning point ◆ I became an enthusiastic change agent ◆ "Think and Do and Solve Problems" was our theme; we discussed empowering people ◆ The final mission statement document ◆ "Management" decided to jump start the program ◆ Lifesaving results ◆ The importance of trust ◆ Opening up our financial statements broke the mold of secrecy ◆ We handled cutting to the bone, "counseling out" and delivering bad news differently ◆ For the next eighteen months, our firm dug its way out of a difficult hole

---

I began our first office-wide meeting with the promise of trying to create an environment where ***people would do things because they wanted to, not because they were afraid not to.***

I told our people I wanted to create a workplace where people looked forward to spending their time. I admitted it had been some time since I had looked forward to coming to work myself and I acknowledged it must have been even worse for everyone else.

Had I heard of core values at that time, I would have realized we had just identified our first one. Indeed, when we wrote our core values in 1995, the first to appear on the list dealt with establishing an environment similar to the one we discussed in 1991.

Although the first meeting was on the idealistic side and a bit euphoric, it should not have been a surprise to anyone that we quickly reverted to the only management style we had ever known--the traditional pyramid. A fear-driven management style prevailed and continued. The attitude was "up or out" and for most people, the "out" was the eventual result. This was standard operating procedure for accounting firms. From February through April 1991, we functioned under this system as we always had. We worked so hard to get through our first busy season no one really noticed a need to make any adjustment in management style, but the need was definitely there.

However, from the beginning, we made some subtle changes.

♦ We formed a management committee comprised of former partners and managers and shifted to making most decisions as a group. The basic rule was, we would discuss issues as a group and seek consensus, but if this proved difficult I would step in as the benevolent dictator and make the decision. This was the beginning of a move toward team decisions and participative management.

♦ We began distributing the firm's financial statements to the members of the management committee. This was the beginning of a move toward open book management.

♦ We changed our titles from six levels (partner, senior manager, manager, senior, senior assistant, assistant) to three (shareholder, senior associate and associate). We stopped referring to our people as two classes--professionals and nonprofessionals. This was the beginning of flattening the organization.

♦ We instituted a casual day on Friday before this was a generally accepted business practice This decision followed many hours of discussing the variety of abuses that could occur and the fear of negative feedback from clients and professional peers.

This demonstrated our willingness to "step out of the box." We suggested people bring their children to work on days that created daycare issues such as Columbus Day, Presidents' Day and in-service training days for teachers--despite fears of disrupting the workplace and complaints from clients. This was the first step toward creating a "family friendly workplace."

Most of these early decisions were more symbolic than substantive.

In summary, these actions demonstrated to us that we were not afraid to break the mold; however, at the time, our people placed no particular significance on any of these actions. We had not yet begun to seriously challenge the traditional culture. In essence, the existing system was only being tweaked, but it was a beginning. We were planting the seeds for significant change.

During these first few months, another significant series of discussions was occurring among the shareholders of the firm. At the time I was 37 and the other two shareholders of the firm were 52 and 53. Before we formed the new firm, we decided I would be the managing shareholder. Although titles are not used on correspondence or business cards, when someone requires a title to introduce me, I now suggest "leading shareholder."

A new direction for the firm was discussed--one that would not replicate our predecessor, Lanier, Locke & Ritter. That firm's culture had been shaped in the sixties and had continued until 1986, when LL&R sold its practice to a Big Six firm. When Lanier, the founder of the firm, retired, Tom Locke and Mark Ritter became partners in the Big Six firm. I moved from Houston to Austin to join the new office.

As the new ML&R was forming in 1991, it was important for people to understand we were not just turning the clock back to 1986.

Indeed, we were committed to doing something quite different. Our goal was to create the ideal local firm of the nineties and beyond. We even incorporated the color teal into our firm logo because someone suggested it would become the color of the nineties. We still joke about this choice of a firm color, especially at firm picnics where the teal colored boat I purchased is still used.

When I tell other professionals the story of our journey toward redefining the firm, the reaction I can always expect is an assumption that my partners must have been either my age or younger. In any event, about thirty minutes into the story people begin to wonder how I got my partners to agree to this new direction.

Most are surprised when I tell them that both of my partners were in their fifties, and probably not very different than their own partners, when we began the journey. Locke and Ritter agreed to this new direction, although I am not sure to what extent they believed in it. Actually, they probably thought it was absolutely crazy. Most importantly, they agreed not to obstruct or sabotage any of the new ideas or efforts.

I am more thankful that, as the new direction became even more radical than I had originally envisioned, they supported me.

In fact, as we continued our journey, they began to actively encourage the changes that were occurring. They are now two of the biggest advocates of change in the office and best spokesmen for the changes that have taken place.

Support from the shareholders was pivotal.

One of our senior associates who has been with the new firm every step of the way made presentations to the local Quality Council. In those presentations, she stressed the importance of having the total commitment of the chief executive officer. I agree this is a critical first step, but we could not have moved our firm in this new direction without the support of my partners. When people ask me how in the world a CPA firm could have moved in this direction, my reply is simple. *My two partners did not keep it from happening and eventually became ardent supporters of the new culture.* In a professional service firm, support at the partner or shareholder level is absolutely critical to a reengineering effort. I am not sure any managing partner or shareholder could overcome another owner's critical opposition to the necessary changes. The changes are extremely difficult-- even with support from the shareholders.

Another important question that follows our presentations concerns the amount of time we spend in meetings. "*What happened to your billable hours?*" they ask in disbelief.

Our response is not what the CPAs in the audience expect. Although the time spent by our staff in meetings has increased to over 200 hours per person per year, billable hours of our associates have increased. Billable shareholder hours have increased. Yet the total hours have remained relatively constant.

The next question is usually, "*How can that be?*"

♦ We have effectively replaced about 200 hours per person of unproductive administrative or unassigned time with productive activities.

♦ The cross functional nature of the teams has done more than anything to help break barriers between the traditional departments.

♦ Our leadership no longer spends 70% of their time complaining about the administrative staff. ***They*** have become ***we***.

♦ Administrative processes are being developed and improved by the consumers of support--the CPAs themselves.

♦ We have 40% fewer administrative people than the typical CPA firm.

After three years of process team activities, I believe the real question should be, ***"Can we afford not to spend so much time in efficiently run process team meetings?"***

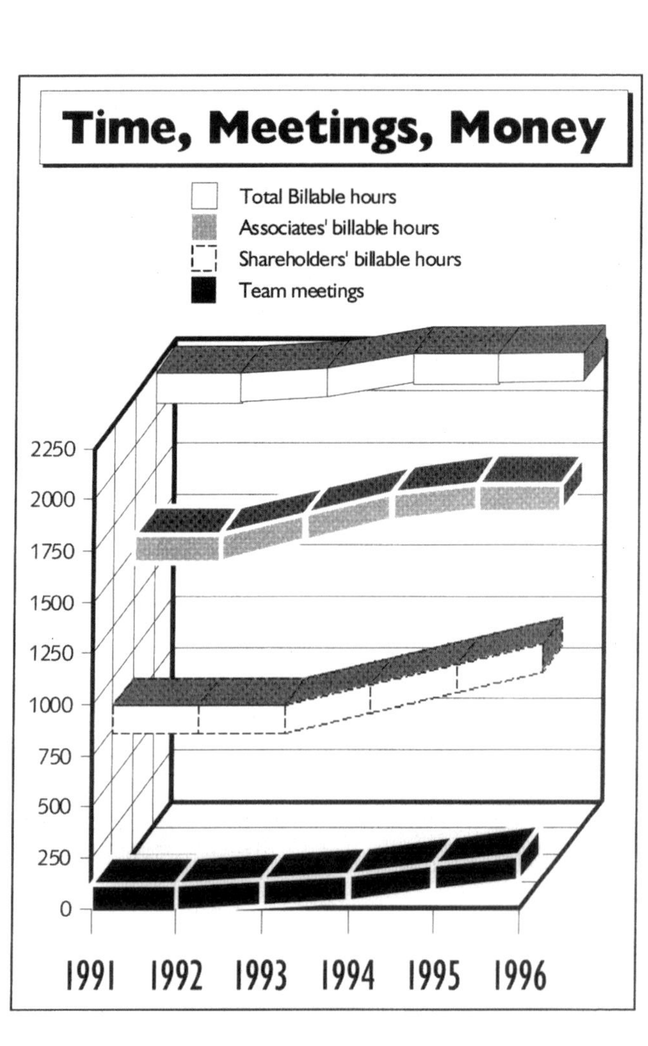
Time, Meetings, Money
Total Billable hours
Associates' billable hours
Shareholders' billable hours
Team meetings
2250
2000
1750
1500
1250
1000
750
500
250
0
1991
1992
1993
1994
1995
1996

Herb Kelleher was one of my earliest mentors from the TQM movement. He was at least twenty years ahead of most of the corporate world.

In August 1991, we moved to our current location. We purchased two signs which continue to be displayed in our office. I ordered them from a gift magazine on a Southwest Airlines flight.

The signs state:

> *"Quality is never an accident; it is always the result of high intention, sincere effort, intelligent direction and skillful execution; it represents the wise choice of many alternatives."*

> *"Excellence can be attained if you...*
> *Care more than others think is wise.*
> *Risk more than others think is safe.*
> *Dream more than others think is practical.*
> *Expect more than others think is possible."*

The appearance of the signs, in and of themselves, was not a big deal. However, their presence constantly reminds us of our renewed commitment to quality and excellence.

An early turning point.

A significant turning point came in September 1991, when I attended a practice management conference sponsored by the American Institute of Certified Public Accountants (AICPA) in Dallas. For three days I listened carefully as the speakers presented the massive changes that were affecting our profession. Most of the predicted impacts were less than positive, at best. An interesting phenomenon occurred when *I began to realize that most of what I was hearing reinforced our firm's earliest decisions.*

I became an enthusiastic change agent.

I returned home and thought about what I had heard. Upon returning to the office I decided it was time to take a plunge.

I once read, "No one's blood was ever stirred by a leader who stood in front of his troops and said, let's dare to be conservative."

We scheduled an all day office-wide meeting for October. Everyone attended, including the support staff, who had previously been referred to as "nonprofessionals." Until then, they had not participated in meetings or social events with "professionals."

"Think and Do and Solve Problems" was the theme of the meeting, our first discussion devoted to the concept of empowering people.

We learned it takes longer than you can imagine for people to begin believing "management" is serious about implementing this concept. Also, we learned how difficult it is for "management" to let go so people can be "empowered."

"Management" sent many confusing signals before learning to relinquish control. I explained what I had heard at the conference and that I was committed to trying some relatively innovative things for an accounting firm.

We discussed contemporary thinking for a progressive firm operating in a traditional industry. We talked of adaptation, management style changes--from pyramid to rectangle--flexible career tracks, technological advances, client-driven (rather than product-driven) efforts, exploding consumer demands, solutions-driven services and niche consulting.

Some of our people thought I had lost my mind; but, on that day I intentionally applied a shock treatment to our group of twenty-two people.

As radical as it seemed at the time, many of the predicted changes to professional service firms occurred during the next five years, at an even faster rate than I expected.

After the shock treatment, I explained we were going to begin by writing a mission statement--*together*. We divided into five groups with instructions for each group to draft a mission statement. Some people seemed surprised by this seeming lack of direction and by the three shareholders not joining any of the groups. We did not know it at the time, but this was one of the most important steps in the journey.

We were doing more than writing a mission statement. We were defining our purpose.

Most importantly, everyone in the firm was participating without the intimidation of shareholders who had traditionally dominated such discussions. After each group presented its mission statement and taped it to the wall, we found two common threads--we care about our clients and each other.

The final mission statement document:

"We provide highest quality solutions and services to clients from an environment which promotes each person's personal goals, self esteem and professionalism."

Since that day the document has been prominently displayed in our office and shown to several hundred visitors. At least thirty officewide meetings have begun with an overhead of the mission statement as constant reinforcement.

Significantly, it began appearing on the walls of individual workstations.

Now that does not sound like much. But remember, we are talking about conservative accountants who do not change easily and are not accustomed to operating in such a manner. There may have been a desire for change, but there was still a very real fear of "management" that had been ingrained in the accounting culture for many years. Looking back, I do not believe many people really expected anything to change. What we did accomplish that day was a milestone.

We defined our purpose. As leading shareholder, I committed my efforts and the resources of our organization to this new direction.

Shortly after the meeting, "management" decided to jump start the program.

After many hours of analyzing our Mission Statement, "management" determined that our people wanted to enhance self esteem and achieve personal goals. So we hired a fellow by the name of Zig Ziglar to help us. Of course, Mr. Ziglar did not personally come to our office, but he sent a wonderful motivational program that consisted of videos, workbooks and exercises. One of our future shareholders, who had received three days of training in the Ziglar approach, led the program. For the next fifteen weeks we met for two hours every Monday morning.

As it turned out, "management" was way off base in believing that the Ziglar program would result in motivating our associates to market the firm and spend more time growing the practice.

The program had some unexpected results.

As people began to settle into the idea of periodic meetings, they slowly dropped their guards and shared personal experiences with the group. *Mutual trust* and *friendship* began to develop across pyramid lines, departments and functions. The process exposed people to accepting *vulnerability*, something that had previously been unacceptable. These group exercises, which seemed ridiculous at the time, encouraged this vulnerability, which later would become so important to our reengineering efforts.

Many of Zig's philosophies about developing and maintaining healthy attitudes continue to be utilized by people who attended the sessions five years ago.

Lifesaving results.

On a personal basis, the program saved my life because it caused me to reflect on things I had not seen while in the fast lane of Big Six public accounting. Accordingly, I made some significant changes to my personal life. Although some thought the $6,000 project was a colossal waste of money, I thought saving my life was worthwhile, even if the firm had not altogether realized its expected benefits!

The importance of trust.

♦ Trust is the most important element that must exist before you can begin to make the cultural transformation described in this book.

♦ Trust can only exist when people reveal enough information about themselves to become vulnerable.

♦ Until "management" accepts and encourages this vulnerability, effective implementation of the concepts discussed in this book will be impossible.

♦ "Management" must do this--*you* must do this. If not, you can forget reengineering, or whatever you choose to call it.

♦ Trust underlies the concepts of open book management, effective team work, strategic alliances, profit sharing and many other ideas discussed in this book.

♦ Unless you can commit to developing mutual trust, you should stick to your traditional style. Anything less than full commitment to a trustful environment is a recipe for disaster.

In early 1992, ML&R communicated one of the biggest secrets of "management" to the entire office. We opened our financial statements and said, "*Here it is, gang. Let's talk about it.*" I have presented hundreds of financial statements to other organizations, but had never been so nervous as I was that day. I refer to it as the day "management" bared its soul to the rest of the office. The financial picture was not pretty and people left the meeting feeling somewhat doomed. I was so relieved to survive, I did not take much time to worry about what others thought of the meeting.

The act of opening up our financial statements broke the mold of secrecy.

The next busy season was dismal. By the end of it, we were $200,000 behind planned revenues, leveraged to the extent of our line of bank credit, in trouble with our lenders and pretty much insolvent. During this time, self esteem and morale took a back seat to survival. I am not certain how we would respond to this situation today, but after a period of depression (at least by the leading shareholder) we decided it was time to make some very difficult decisions.

On a Friday afternoon, one of my partners grabbed my attention with a serious discussion of our grave situation and reminded me of my responsibility to take charge.

This reminder probably saved our firm.

Here is what we did.

- Restructured our debt after painful discussions with our lenders.
- Reduced each shareholder's annual salary by $18,000 and agreed to forego two months pay.
- Relinquished shareholders' club memberships and paid parking.
- Reduced operating expenses by $25,000.
- Reduced leased office space by 600 square feet.
- Fired three associates (counseled out, down sized, terminated--whatever.)

We handled a difficult situation differently in a couple of respects.

During the process, a lengthy discussion ensued concerning the size of the severance packages offered. Some shareholders argued we should offer severance in the same amounts as an international accounting firm, along with out-placement counseling.

Others reminded the group we were not an international accounting firm, reinforced by the fact that we were broke. Now, the *mission statement* entered the scene. Someone reminded the shareholder group of the part of our statement that focused on the importance of caring for our own people. The tide of the discussion turned, and we decided to offer severance packages equivalent to those offered by an international firm. Shareholders forfeited two months' salaries, since we had no money and we had exhausted our credit.

Next, we communicated our decisions with the individuals affected. After so much time spent improving morale, this was extremely difficult. I still have trouble speaking about it.

The next morning, we had an officewide meeting with the remaining seventeen people. We discussed the dismal financial position of the firm. We took great care to emphasize that the people leaving the firm would have access to their offices and the resources of the firm until they found another job. We asked that everyone in the room do whatever they could to assist in these job searches. Finally, we focused on the survivors and thanked them for staying with us through this difficult journey. I said something to the effect that there must be a pony in here somewhere, and assured everyone we would keep looking for it. I had learned that familiar story from one of my partners.

The communication-at-large was significant, since it set a new direction for delivering bad news.

Our traditional culture believed associates were not really capable of handling bad news. Truthfully, we did not communicate bad news for fear the rats would flee a sinking ship. Similarly, firings were not openly communicated. Instead, people mysteriously disappeared from the audit schedule or due date monitoring list. Sometimes, a notice appeared on the bulletin board announcing the new position accepted by the former employee or simply that someone had left the firm "to pursue other interests."

Two or three days after the meeting, one of my partners told me he originally thought my idea of openly communicating was questionable, but had now decided it had been the right thing to do. I have never told him how much this encouragement meant to me.

During this difficult time, I sought the counsel of my father, who had been a small businessman all his life.

His advice was sage:

"Business is really pretty simple. Your firm cannot continue spending more than it makes. If you cannot afford to grant raises or pay bonuses, be honest with your people and tell them the truth. Do this even if you have promised the raises or bonuses. Draw the line. Do not borrow any more money just for the sake of living up to the unrealistic economic expectations of your people."

Over the next eighteen months, our firm dug its way out of a difficult hole. (I have never understood how anyone can dig their way out of a hole. It seems as if the hole would keep getting deeper.) In any event, we eventually surfaced.

In the meantime, I learned what it feels like to wake up in a cold sweat at 4:00 in the morning knowing we were only two days from payday and $30,000 short. Thank God we had people who called clients for payment and we had clients who graciously wrote the checks and told us we could come pick them up. During this period of time we often made mad dashes between phone calls, client locations and the bank. Through it all, we never failed to make payroll, but we endured many close calls. *I am very thankful for the people who worked so hard during this time and sacrificed so much.* It really was an incredible effort.

Chapter 3. Beginning the Conversion-- Seizing the Benefits of Outside Help

◆ Close encounters with an outside influence ◆ His presentation wasn't a presentation at all ◆ We were about to screw up our plan ◆ We felt like the frog in a pot of water, when the heat was being gradually increased ◆ Karl Krumm wasn't preaching, he was teaching ◆ He frustrated us by not telling us what to do ◆ We were asking the right questions ◆ Expanding the definition of customers ◆ Negatives of compensation and recognition systems ◆ Shaking the sack of performance-based systems ◆ A new way of establishing goals ◆ Understanding the cost of rework ◆ Rework from a Japanese point of view ◆ Rework costs painted a perfect picture of public accounting practices for the last half a century ◆ Early attempts to change our traditional thinking

---

By the summer of 1993, the financial position of the firm was improving, along with the local economy. We continued to have a sound client base and decent service delivery. We were well positioned in the marketplace and still confident this quality thing could work.

Then we came to another critical point.

When we began the TQM journey in 1991, I believed it would take about two years to convert from the traditional organizational model to something new and exciting. However, two years had passed and our progress had been excruciatingly slow. I told one of the senior associates I was disappointed that we were two years down the road and only 30 percent of the way toward achieving the kind of culture we envisioned. The senior associate told me he had recently attended a leadership conference and the presenter was someone I should meet. He suggested that Karl Krumm sounded a lot like me, but he really knew what he was talking about.

An outside influence might be able to hasten our progress in creating the organizational culture we sought, he suggested. This was significant to me because this particular senior associate had not been an apparent proponent of the new direction; however, he cared enough to bring this to my attention.

Close encounters with an outside influence.

We arranged a meeting and arrived at Karl Krumm's office. I took my place on the couch and must admit I was uncomfortable in this very clinical setting.

No one had told me Karl was a psychologist.

He introduced himself as an organizational consultant trained as a clinical psychologist. This was supposed to make me feel better. The consummate professional, Karl encouraged me to tell our story, which I could not do without expressing frustration.

At the conclusion of the meeting, we agreed the next step would be for Karl to spend an afternoon with our management group to determine if an ongoing relationship would be mutually beneficial. I told Karl I would prefer to introduce him to the group on a first name basis. If they liked him, I would eventually tell them he was a clinical psychologist. Until then, I feared this knowledge would be counter-productive, as accountants were probably the last to seek the advice of a shrink. He agreed with this approach and we proceeded.

His presentation wasn't a presentation at all.

Karl came into the conference room armed with a milk carton full of overhead transparencies in no apparent order. Immediately, I was uncomfortable with what seemed like a somewhat disorganized presentation. My Big Six experience taught me to expect well prepared, seemingly "canned" presentations that used the latest technology. Most presentations focused on facts and solutions, but Karl's teaching style focused on concepts and questions. For example, when noise from an antique overhead projector distracted us, Karl unplugged the projector between slides so we could carry on a conversation. I explained we had not had a capital expenditures budget for several years, but I was still embarrassed. The next week we bought a new projector. Karl still asks about the old one.

We were about to screw up our plan.

In this four hour session, Karl told us we had started something he believed was unique for an accounting firm. However, he convinced us we probably could not finish the project without some help. The session was low key but dynamic, and the group agreed that we really needed Karl's assistance. This relieved me because I knew we had come too far to go back to our old ways.

Another important discussion was ensuing during the time we were becoming acquainted with Karl. Our management group was truly becoming convinced that unless we made dramatic changes to our organization, we would be dead in five to ten years. Although enough would be left to provide some people a living, our firm, as we had known it, would not continue to exist.

We felt like the frog in a pot of water, when the heat was being gradually increased.

Over a period of time the frog is comfortable and does not detect that the water is warming. In this situation, the frog eventually boils to death--a slow and tolerable death, but death nonetheless. However, when a frog is dropped into a pot of boiling water, he immediately jumps out and survives. The more we studied our situation and the changes occurring in the business sector, the more we believed it was time to turn up the heat and jump out of the pot. Although there was plenty of risk associated with jumping out of the pot, everyone agreed we were not ready to die a slow death.

Within a few weeks of our original meeting with Karl, we introduced him to the entire office. For the first ten minutes of his presentation he demonstrated that "management" had misapplied TQM. This demonstration was a humbling experience to "management," but the rest of the office probably enjoyed it. They were in an "I told you so" mood.

Karl Krumm wasn't preaching, he was teaching.

Then Karl began the healing process. This was a particularly important session for me because it became apparent Karl was more effective at teaching the concepts than I. For two years my attempt at teaching had usually come across as preaching. Now people were listening and nodding. Since I was not under the pressure of being on stage, I was able to sit back and observe responses to the concepts being discussed.

Karl brought academic credibility that reinforced many of the things we had haphazardly attempted. We were CPAs attempting significant changes to our organization without professional help. None of us could disguise ourselves as organizational consultants. My thinking had been shaped by books and audio tapes. However, Karl had probably forgotten more TQM and Deming-based concepts than I had ever read or heard. Karl said many of the same things we had said, but he said them in a more credible and confident manner. The other important asset Karl brought to our learning was a nonthreatening and casual teaching style.

He frustrated us by not telling us what we should do.

We were accustomed to well organized slide shows and a more formal style of training than Karl offered. Instead, he came to the meetings with several overhead transparencies and a general idea of what we were attempting to accomplish. In a very casual way, he started with a transparency and talked about it for a while. Instead of offering solutions, he asked questions. Instead of answering our questions, he encouraged us to ask questions among ourselves. When he sensed a particular response to what we had seen or heard, he encouraged discussion. Then he moved to another transparency until the next response led him to facilitate another discussion among our group. He would then move to another concept.

Eventually discussion among the group became so free flowing that he stepped out of it altogether. Sometimes he stepped away for ten minutes--sometimes for forty-five minutes. Then he stepped in and we moved to another concept. By the end of the session we generally accomplished our training goals, but rarely in the order or the fashion I expected.

We were asking the right questions.

When pressed for a solution, he responded that we were asking the right questions. He assured us that if we asked the right questions, we were on the way to developing our own solutions. The closest he came to complimenting us was in telling us most companies were not even asking the right questions. Also, there were times he shocked us by telling us we were light years away from accomplishing our desired goals. He told us we really did not seem committed to making the difficult fundamental changes. These teaching styles were shaped by his training as a clinical psychologist and they were effective. Around the office these meetings became known as ***"Krumm Sessions."***

As Karl continued to work with us, he introduced Deming's basic concepts. As our group began to understand the concepts, we began to search for practical applications. Some of the earliest ideas that had significant impact on our firm included a new way of defining customers; a discussion of compensation, bonus and recognition systems; a new way of establishing goals; and gaining a new understanding of rework. Each of these discussions attacked and tore down some of our firm's most sacred beliefs and foundations.

Expanding the definition of customers.

We were introduced to the concept of expanding the traditional definition of a customer to include both external and internal customers. Many of our people had never thought of each other as customers. However, as we began to understand Deming's concepts of internal customers, we began to look at and treat each other differently. Later this understanding allowed us to better analyze processes and appreciate their impact on our people. Each person began to think about who the internal customers were for each task performed. The impact of expanding the definition of customers to include our own people was profound. Ultimately it allowed us to understand the extent to which every task performed was interconnected with many other tasks, processes and systems.

Acknowledging the negatives of compensation and recognition systems.

Karl introduced us to some of the negative by-products of most traditional compensation and recognition systems. Quite frankly, we had never given much thought to the negative by-products of some of our most sacred practices. However, during the first several months of the Krumm Sessions, Karl did an excellent job of encouraging us to question some of the systems we took for granted. One of the first questions he asked was, "Who is the most hated and despised person in most companies?" Our responses were not even close to the answer he desired. Finally, he showed us a picture of a reserved parking space for the "Employee of the Month." Most of us laughed. Most employees surveyed would rather have almost anything happen to them than to receive this recognition. However, management and human resource directors continue to motivate their employees by silly recognition exercises such as "Employee of the Month." What an unbelievable situation.

Shaking the sack of performance based systems.

Next, Karl discussed some of the negative by-products of performance based bonus systems. He explained that many of these systems included formula driven bonuses, sales commissions and goal setting. He provided example after example of the negative effects of these traditional compensation systems. Most organizations never discuss the internal competition caused by performance based bonus systems. These formula-driven systems encouraged people to focus on their own personal statistics and the resulting compensation. As a result, people's efforts are driven by statistics rather than company goals. Worse, many of the formulas contradict and compete with the company's overall strategies.

Although Karl had no direct knowledge of the ML&R compensation and recognition systems, his discussion struck very close to home. *It took us quite a while to fully accept these premises and take the risk of abandoning some of our sacred beliefs.*

A new way of establishing goals.

We began to explain to Karl our annual goal setting and performance review processes. We had been very proud of them. Karl provided more examples of goal setting processes that established ceilings people rarely surpassed--even when the ability existed. With much resistance from his audience, he began to steer our thinking toward Deming's concepts. We began to question a culture that continued to cling to individual goal setting prescribed by the old *management by objectives* (MBO) system. Slowly but surely we grasped the concepts Karl discussed.

Eventually, we replaced our goal setting process with a new approach--one which began with the firm determining its "Aim." The Aim responded to the question of what our firm is attempting to become. Next, the firm developed strategic directives which responded to the question of how we were going to accomplish the Aim. The system was drawn as a wide body arrow pointed up toward the Aim. Within the body of the arrow resided the strategic directives necessary to accomplish the Aim.

Individuals determined their roles in contributing to the firm's strategic directives--with full knowledge of the firm's ultimate Aim. Finally, we went to work on aligning the internal processes and systems of the firm with the Aim. As we approached this effort, it became apparent many of our sacred systems did not really fit within and support the overall Aim of our firm. We began to change or replace some of these systems. Only then could we create a firm in which the processes adequately supported its strategic directives and activities.

We determined our Aim:

- ***Become the preferred business advisors of our clients;***
- ***Work less and make more;***
- ***Ensure our firm's long-term viability.***

Understanding the cost of rework.

Karl introduced the concept of rework. He began this session by saying most companies accepted between 20 percent and 30 percent of rework as a cost of doing business. Most companies do not realize the extent of rework because they have not closely examined the interconnected processes. He asked how much rework existed in our office.

Most everyone agreed our situation was "much better than the average bear's." We believed this because our definition of rework revolved around audit reports reissued or tax returns amended because of mistakes made on our part. Indeed, these situations were rare.

Karl then drew two graphs to illustrate a point. The graphs were each dated in the mid-seventies and involved the costs of building cars in Japan, contrasted with those built in the United States. The X axis of the graph represented the timeline of building a car. It was labeled product design and planning, manufacturing, quality control and factory recalls. The Y axis represented the cost of building a car. The Japanese graph showed significant costs incurred during product design and planning. The U.S. graph showed a much smaller cost incurred during this phase of the process. The costs incurred during the manufacturing phase were similar for each of the countries. To the right of the graph, the Japanese spent very little on quality control or factory recalls. The U.S. prided itself in quality control systems and spent far more than the Japanese in this area. Then why did the U.S. spend so much on factory recalls when the Japanese spent almost nothing? Finally, why was the total cost of production in Japan less than the cost in the U.S.?

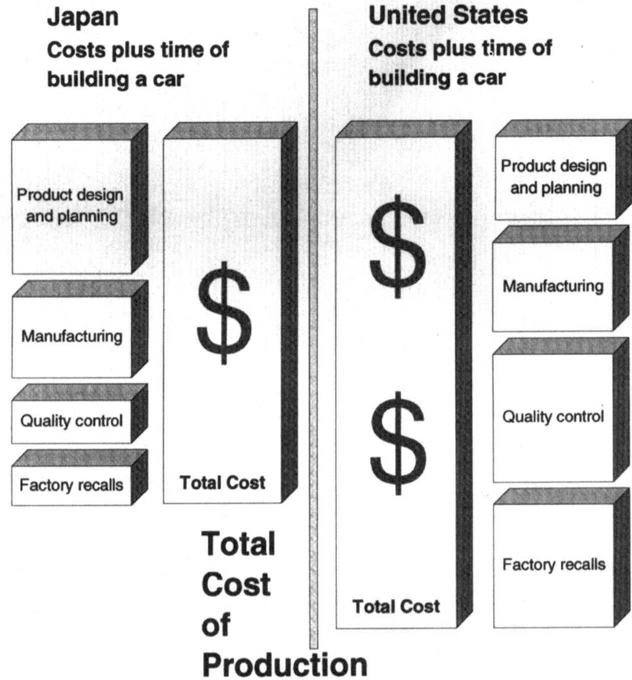

Rework from a Japanese point of view.

At first we believed the answers to these questions somehow related to lower salary costs in Japan. Karl explained the graphs had been adjusted to eliminate payroll differences. Another focused on the importance of planning any project and suggested the cost of planning was significantly less than the cost of factory recalls. We were warming to the occasion.

Then someone observed the cost of rework was always expensive. No one addressed the question of why Japan spent almost nothing on quality control. Karl helped us by steering the conversation toward processes. Then someone suggested the Japanese built their quality control function into their manufacturing process. Someone else argued they even incorporated quality control considerations into their planning and design processes. Now we were really fired up about the concepts. The bottom line was that by reversing the curve and spending time and money on the front end of a project, *total costs were reduced.*

This was a significant part of the answer to why the Japanese were "beating our car manufacturers' brains out" during the seventies and early eighties. This was also why Dr. Deming's philosophies had finally become accepted by the U.S. car manufacturers during the eighties. Prior to this he had been exiled to work with Japanese companies for thirty to forty years. He had journeyed to Japan after World War II because U.S. companies thought his manufacturing philosophies were unsound.

The discussion of rework painted a perfect picture of public accounting practices in this country for the last half a century.

When Karl moved to another slide, someone asked him to return to the slide showing the two graphs. That person suggested that the U.S. graph was a perfect picture of public accounting practices in this country for the last forty or fifty years. We spent little time planning our projects and lots of time in the quality control process--known as three or four layers of review and volumes of review notes. Someone else defended this as the way our younger people learned. Another person countered that if the review process occurred in the field, or on the manufacturing floor (if you will), not as many review notes would be necessary. They also suggested that if management spent more time in the planning process, perhaps the execution of the project could or might be more efficient.

We concluded most of our review and quality control processes represented rework built into the system. By the end of the session our definition of rework had significantly expanded. Now, we began to wonder if our system might have twenty to thirty percent of rework built into it--disguised as review and quality control. We began to wonder about the efficiencies that would occur if we reversed the curve.

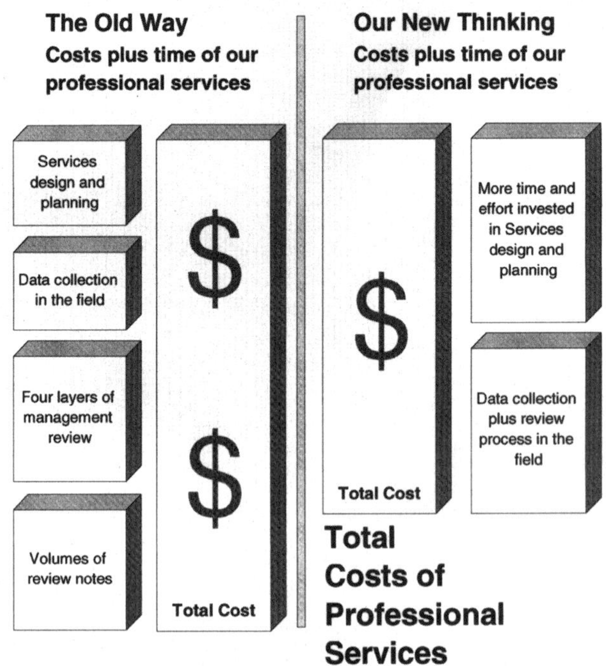

Examples of our early attempts to change our traditional thinking.

By September, we had established four process teams.

1. The **Technology Team's** responsibility was to review and improve our processes through the use of technology. This included our computer network, hardware, software, phone system, voice mail, fax machine and copy machines.

2. The **Common Area Team's** responsibility was to examine and improve the processes of our common areas such as the reception area, library, conference room, kitchen, file room and hallways. These processes included the manner in which our phones were answered, visitors greeted, library materials updated, conference room and kitchen maintained and file room organized.

3. The **Marketing-Client Service Team's** responsibility was to examine and improve our client service delivery and marketing activities. This cycle included the manner in which we marketed our services, responded to opportunities, presented proposals, accepted new clients, performed the services, delivered our products, billed and collected fees, and finally were rehired to perform next year's services.

4. The **Human Resource Team's** responsibility was to improve the environment in which our people worked. Areas of focus included fringe benefits, counseling, performance evaluation, firm social events and continuing professional education.

Although participation on any of these teams was one hundred percent voluntary, we had one hundred percent participation. Once the teams were established, parameters were given to each, concerning the nature of their responsibilities.

Things began to happen.

Ideas that had been tossed around for the past two years suddenly became the vision of the team and within months, sometimes within days, those ideas became reality. The transformation was beginning to speed up! For the next year Karl facilitated officewide sessions every other month and met with several of the process teams to help them overcome implementation hurdles. By 1995, the officewide meetings took place on a quarterly basis as the cultural changes began to accelerate.

Chapter 4. Improving Communication Through Open Book Management

♦ Removing the mystery surrounding the firm's financial statements ♦ Communicating the firm's financial highlights to the entire office each month ♦ Opening up communications even more ♦ Exposing financial losses was painful ♦ A meeting where I could not speak. They did. It worked! ♦ Profit sharing instead of performance-based bonuses ♦ Our people joined in developing the annual operating plan ♦ Revising the distribution of financial results ♦ Tremendous strides in practicing open communication, even when it is difficult ♦ Every plan was completed by the assigned time ♦ Benefits to open book management far outweigh any problems caused by it ♦ Implementation of this concept has enabled us to live the core values of the firm

---

Our earliest attempts at cranking up the communication effort mirrored by two statements I later read: "We routinely underestimate the amount of communication necessary to make our efforts successful," and "Make sure everyone knows the business. It's easy when you don't know how, but very difficult when you do."

From the earliest days of the firm we committed to opening the lines of communication.

We discussed the importance of people knowing more about the strategies and operating results of the firm than they had in the past. We began this process by including the entire office in periodic meetings where we discussed plans and reviewed operating results.

We formed a management committee comprised of the shareholders and senior associates of the firm. The management committee of seven people began functioning as a team. In this phase we began learning to make decisions as a group. Previously, individuals made decisions and then got others to "buy into the plan."

An important step was to remove the mystery surrounding the firm's financial statements.

To do this, we began distributing and discussing the firm's monthly financial statements with the entire management committee. The management committee began receiving billing information for the entire office. This included listings of aged accounts receivable, work in process, productivity analyses for every individual and production by function. In the past, each person received information only in areas of their immediate responsibility--under the theory of only communicating the information a manager needed to know.

Another step was to communicate the firm's financial highlights to the entire office each month.

In a very short period of time everyone in our office knew more about the firm's plans and operating results than most partners in Big Six accounting firms. This was a major step.

The prior culture restricted full and open communication of financial information to owners of the firm. For us, it had been *managing partners*. In September 1991, I mentioned this open communications concept to a group of managing partners of local firms at an AICPA conference. It became apparent this was not an accepted practice at most local firms. They warned me of serious consequences that would arise from this action. Some predicted I would abandon it within a short period of time. I thanked everyone for their advice and concern, but held steadfast to this new, if somewhat scary, approach.

Tradition-minded professionals warned against it; I opened up communications even more.

At the firm retreat in October 1991, which was described in Chapter 2, we began to communicate like never before. Then in early 1992, we opened the financial statements to the entire firm. We did it by reviewing the past year's financial results and the 1992 operating plan in detail.

We limited this review to overhead transparencies. We had neither the nerve nor the trust in our own people to distribute hard copies. As a matter of fact, I probably moved to the next transparency before anyone had time to take too many notes. Nonetheless, it was a major step. In hindsight, we were probably driven by a desire to awaken everyone to the reality of our dire financial situation rather than to introduce "open book management"--a term that had not even entered our vocabulary in 1992. Interestingly, the decision to frighten everyone into reality resulted in little or no beneficial action. If anything, people became paralyzed. The days seemed longer and the skies overcast; there was a collective posture of waiting for someone else to come to the rescue. When Superman didn't show, everyone positioned themselves to survive the ultimate down-sizing.

Open communications and exposing financial losses were painful. Still, we kept to it.

As difficult as it was, we continued this level of communication each month from 1991 through 1993. During this period we never achieved our annual financial operating plan and lost over $135,000. For me, preparing for each monthly communication of operating results was like having teeth pulled. However, by January 1994, we had made enough progress in our overall reengineering efforts that we called our annual office meeting the "*First Annual Stakeholders' meeting.*" We achieved this confidence because we sensed a spirit of ownership that had not existed before. I even distributed hard copies of financial statements, along with copies of the overhead transparencies from which I spoke. By now people were interacting instead of just taking notes and nodding. This was progress and others sensed it as well.

As 1994 came to a close, another significant event occurred. The local economy had been in recovery for over a year, but we continued in a cost containment mode. Our audit practice had become the fastest growing part of our firm. However, since it produced the lowest profit margins, we had not hired enough people to do the required work. As a result, we had a staff of auditors who were terribly overworked.

We had a meeting led by Karl Krumm. I could not speak. They did. It worked!

In an officewide meeting led by Karl Krumm, the dissatisfaction came to the surface. I had laryngitis and could barely whisper, which fortunately allowed everyone else to speak their minds. And speak their minds they did. It was the best exchange of information among a group of 25 accountants I had ever witnessed. Although some were threatened by the exchange, I was delighted.

Finally, I posed a question on a hand written note:

"Would you rather get through another four months with the present number of people and level of work, or hire three people?"

Hiring the people would reduce annual net income by $120,000 and significantly reduce the amount of everyone's bonus. The group voted almost unanimously to hire the three people.

We had never exchanged ideas so freely.

This was the first time the entire office had participated in determining an appropriate head count. The answer reinforced something I had heard at an Accounting Firms Associated, inc. (AFAi) Conference, which drove home the differences in values among those who lived through the Depression, the Baby Boomers and Generation X:

- **The Depression Generation lived to work.**
- **The Boomers worked to live.**
- **The Xers lived to live.**

Profit sharing instead of performance based bonuses--What a concept!

In late 1994, the Human Resource Team recommended to the office that we abandon the performance based bonus plan for associates and shareholders. In its place they recommended an officewide profit sharing plan. Everyone in the office would participate -- shareholders, associates, support staff, part-timers and college interns. At the end of each year, 50 percent of accrual based net income would be distributed to everyone in the office. The percentage, obtained by dividing the amount available by total base salaries, would be applied to everyone's base salary to determine their individual profit sharing check. If the resulting percentage was twelve percent, each person received that percentage of their base salary. Chapter 11 is devoted to the intricacies of this concept. For the time being, we will discuss the impact this decision had on the open book management of the firm.

Profit sharing forced us to change significantly the way we developed financial operating plans and the degree to which we discussed financial decisions. Profit sharing became effective in January, 1995. By April, I began to hear people complaining they had no meaningful input in developing the financial operating plan. We began to question certain expenses such as plant maintenance services, business lunches, memberships, contributions, etc. This really came to a head when I heard someone complain about the $48 we had spent on pizza for junior high students visiting our office for Career Day. This one really upset me.

I felt like shucking the whole profit sharing idea. I generally have lots of patience, but little when it comes to nitpicking. After I cooled off, however, I agreed that although the complaining was misguided, it made an important point: ***Profit sharing would not be effective until our people joined in the development of our annual operating plan.***

Then, it would be important to increase their participation in monitoring the budget. When actual results differed from those budgeted, it would be important to involve the office in the decisions necessary to respond to these situations.

In May, the entire office met for our midyear review of operations. I discussed my frustrations with the early implementation of profit sharing. I admitted it had been a mistake to implement profit sharing without changing the way the financial operating plan had been developed. Since 1991, the firm's internal accountant and I spent considerable time each December running the numbers. These were presented to the management team at a planning retreat.

After a follow up meeting or two with the management team, revisions were made and the financial plan was finalized in mid-January. Although much time was spent building the annual plan, the management team spent less than a combined four hours discussing it before approving it.

It was a mistake not including more of the office in the budgeting process. However, I compensated by sharing, with the entire office, more detail about the budgeting process and the budget results than I ever had before.

Also, I committed to involving every process team in building the 1996 financial operating plan, as well as the strategic business plan upon which it was built. After the meeting, complaints and micro-management subsided and we began to focus once again on strategic implementation--not on the price of pizzas.

We revised the distribution of financial results.

We began distributing monthly financial statements to the **Noname** (Leadership) Team and to senior associates who did not serve on the Noname Team. Now we distributed financial results to fourteen people (four shareholders, six senior associates, one associate, one part-time associate and two support staff). The remainder of the office received a one page summary of financial and operating highlights each month.

In hindsight, it seems a bit ridiculous not to have distributed the financial statements to everyone. I guess we had to hang onto something from the past.

I continue to provide an oral State-of-the-Firm presentation to the entire office on a bimonthly basis. Unlike the earlier presentations, I am now very comfortable exposing myself to this vulnerability. I rarely worry about how to say things to the group. I just say it and hope for the best. I have become comfortable introducing concepts to the office before we have developed more than the first or second steps of implementation.

I have learned, "*The journey of a thousand miles begins with the first step.*" Someone has to make the decision to start the trip, though, and incorporating too many people too soon can create all sorts of road blocks.

Our firm has made tremendous strides in practicing open communication, even when it is difficult.

Like most professional service firms, our old style of communication was rigid and controlled. We had to have the recipe written and published before unveiling to the group our idea of baking a cake. Now, there is a sense of spontaneity and openness. We decide to bake a cake; we make sure someone will eat it when we are finished. We look in the pantry to see if we have most of the ingredients. Upon determining that we do, we announce the project to the entire firm. *We are going to bake a cake.* We believe we have the ingredients and the skills to bake something that will taste pretty good. Someone heats the oven. If we have overlooked a necessary ingredient, we have confidence someone will run to the store. Off we go! During the process, the flavor, size or shape of the cake may change, but our objective of baking a tasty cake will not.

Traditional management--attempts to control the uncontrollable instead of adapting to it--is quickly being displaced by teams of workers and leaders with a drastically different operating philosophy. Their individual values are important to them, but they also recognize the benefit of teamwork. Truth, trust and personal responsibility are tools of the new trade. Managers in the quickly-changing business environment concentrate on giving their teams what they need to be able to move and adapt, rather than resist change. This requires open communication that jumps outside the traditional barriers that passed information through layers of hierarchy.

On the first Thursday of every month, everyone is invited to a lunch meeting in our conference room where we share information, express concerns and discuss process issues, bottlenecks, etc. This provides an effective forum for informal communication of firm activities. Simple process related issues are resolved without a process team's involvement. Other more complicated issues which surface during the lunches are assigned to an appropriate process team.

We continue to meet four or five times a year with our organizational consultant, Karl Krumm, to discuss the way we approach our work, how we interact and how we can function as a team to im prove the performance of the firm.

In December 1995, the process teams may have gotten more than they expected. They were assigned the responsibility for building their own process team strategic plans and budgets.

First, each team was asked to list its accomplishments in 1995. Next, teams were asked to list and prioritize their strategies for 1996, with completion dates and resource requirements. Finally, they were furnished account analyses of 1995 spending levels in their respective areas and asked to complete expected spending levels in 1996.

To facilitate this assignment, each team was furnished basic assumptions for the 1996 operating plan. These included officewide projections of revenue and number of full-time and part-time people. Teams were assigned various account analyses:

1. **Technology Team**
   Computer repairs and maintenance
   Software
   Capital spending - computers, voice mail, scanners, remote access, etc.

2. **Common Area Team**
   Office supplies
   Kitchen
   Printing
   Plant care
   Postage and express mail delivery service

3. Human Resources Team
Medical and dental insurance
Professional dues and licenses
401(k) contributions
Professional development
Workmen's compensation
Professional and trade associations
Firm meetings

4. Marketing and Client Service Team
Advertising
Newsletter
Meals and entertainment
Other practice development
Marketing

5. Noname Team (Leadership Team)
Community contributions
Revenue estimates
Compile operating plan
Approve operating plan

6. Shareholders
Establish base salaries

7. Every Individual
Develop head count projections by completing individual time commitments

This approach involved virtually everyone in the office. Completed information was expected within three weeks of the assignment so team leaders could present team plans to the Noname Team.

Much to my surprise, every plan was completed by the assigned time.

This was affirmation that during the past three years we had learned to function in small teams. The quality of the information presented was *spectacular.* Innovation and creativity dominated each strategic plan. An understanding of the firm's overall strategic directives was clearly demonstrated in each of the plans. I have never been more proud of, or more satisfied with, one of our firm's changes than I have been of our progress toward open book management.

In late 1996, the planning process for 1997 was elevated to a strategic level that surpassed that of the first year of involvement by the process teams. As remarkable as our first year's effort was, it was still pretty much a rote process. There was only a limited amount of strategic thinking that went into planning. Most of the discussions were along the lines of "increase that line by four percent; decrease that line by three percent; do the numbers work?" and "do we really need to pay someone to water the plants?"

However, this year the process teams, and ultimately the Noname Team, pushed the dynamics of the planning process to a new level.

Most importantly, discussions revolved around how we expected to prioritize our spending and investing, to enable us to achieve our strategic directives. Discussions of what we expected to achieve in 1997 were followed by discussions of how next year's achievements will impact strategic directives of 1998 and beyond.

We closed 1996 with the demonstrated ability of the process teams and the Noname Team to think and interact strategically.

This is timely because I believe the next two years will be pivotal for our firm. We are positioned to take several new products to our marketplace. We are also ready to begin addressing nontraditional pricing strategies and the implementation of a call management process.

Our ability to freely interact with each other on these issues will allow our teams to function as "think tanks" for innovative and creative solutions and strategies. This is what we really had in mind when we accepted open book management as a way of life. Now, it is coming to fruition.

Before summarizing the benefits of open book management, there are exceptions we should point out. Obviously, we are bound to confidentiality about client matters. We will not violate any member's confidence on a personal matter--including recruiting negotiations with people who are considering joining the firm.

We will not disclose the details of prospective practice acquisitions--such disclosure could cause irreparable damage to the respective parties. Also, we reserve major investment decisions, which have the potential of changing the face of the firm, to the shareholder group. There have been three or four of those events during the past six years.

Finally, we have not disclosed individual salaries to anyone outside the shareholder group. However, these topics are discussed in general terms--we are interviewing people; we are negotiating the purchase of another practice; we are attempting to resolve a sensitive matter; etc.

In summary, the benefits of open book management far outweigh any problems caused by it.

Frequently, when I present the idea of open book management to executives who have not been converted, I am asked if we have had a disappointing year since we began sharing the firm's financial results with everyone in the firm. Someone usually tells of a situation with which they are familiar where a company abandoned open book management because of negative experiences they had when results went south.

Although I cannot speak to these situations and we have not had a bad year since 1993, we have had many months in which our results fell far short of our operating plan. In these situations, our people have not panicked or feared for their jobs. Instead, they have responded in positive ways to our failure to meet short term goals. Some executives either do not believe this, or discount our experience as not having met the test of time. However, all I know is what I have experienced and it has been most positive.

Implementation of this concept has enabled us to live the core values of the firm.

Obviously, it has encouraged open communication. People complete tasks because they want to, not because they are afraid not to. It has encouraged the concept of *commitment.* When leadership openly communicates its commitment to the firm's initiatives, people are more inclined to commit themselves individually.

Open communication means having to discuss our firm's failures as well as our successes. When the failures of the firm or its leadership are regularly communicated, individuals are less fearful of communicating their own failures. This lessens the risk of leadership asking after the fact, "Why didn't you tell me sooner about this?"

Open communication is a prerequisite to treating everyone with honesty, dignity and respect, and it is the first step towards encouraging our people to treat each other and our clients in a similar manner.

Ultimately, this openness leads everyone to do unto others as we would have others do unto us. Most importantly, open book management instills trust within the organization and supports the teamwork that is central to the theme of this book.

Chapter 5. Maximizing Efforts of the Emerging Work Force

♦ During this transitional period, much of the corporate contract changed ♦ Some of these changes are quite disturbing ♦ Adapting to the needs, aspirations and goals of Generation X ♦ Fear of losing either money or security does not motivate Generation Xers to work harder ♦ What Xers want is respect, challenge and recognition ♦ Personal responsibility is a by-product of the new work ethic ♦ Young people should prepare to live to be 100 ♦ New work habits for a radically changing world ♦ The by-products of our changed culture are better people, lower turnover and higher adaptability for the future

---

Many of the topics discussed in this book result from rapidly changing technologies, increased consumer demands and globalization. However, much of the discussion is driven by an emerging workforce whose habits, values and work ethics bear little resemblance to those of today's managers and executives.

Today's managers grew up in the industrial age where the traditional concepts of management, developed and refined since the industrial revolution, worked fairly effectively. The corporate contract was driven by money, security, status, entitlement, defined retirement plans and the need to control. Loyalty was a by-product of the contract and was expected by both parties.

The emerging workforce (Generation X) grew up and received its college education during the transition from the industrial to the information age.

During this transitional period, much of the corporate contract changed. Some of these changes are quite disturbing.

1. The concept of compensation has moved from one based on seniority and loyalty to one based on recent output--the degree to which an individual contributed to the goals of the corporation last year.

The value of past service diminished and the attitude has become one of "What have you done for us lately?" With this shift came corporate downsizing and all its victims.

2. Guaranteed defined retirement plans have been replaced with 401(k) plans and various unqualified benefit plans.

These new plans provide no guarantees and rely on employees to provide for most of their own retirement funding.

3. Social Security has become a question mark in most younger people's minds.

What social contract? What security? Most people, especially younger people, do not believe that Social Security will be providing benefits to them in retirement.

4. The status and comfort to which management believed itself entitled were removed from the contract.

The previous concept of management, revolving as it did around control and limited access to information, gave way to a new idea of leadership that closely resembled coaching and that recognized the importance of sharing information with those outside management circles. The comforts afforded traditional managers eroded. The new participatory management system requires managers to roll up their sleeves, relinquish reserved parking spaces, move from window offices and fly coach with their staff.

Technology brought information to many people instead of to the select few in management whose power had previously rested within this information. A consumer revolution resulted in an expectation of better quality products delivered faster and at a lower cost.

5. Finally, members of Generation X grew up being told they were the first generation of Americans whose standard of living would not exceed their parents'.

These factors and other changes in society contributed to significant changes in the way people viewed employment and life in general. This was especially pronounced for the group of people called Generation X.

Adapting to the needs, aspirations and goals of Generation X.

I believe and accept the changes that have occurred. A picture on my desk is a constant reminder: "We cannot direct the wind, but we can adjust the sails."

This book, and particularly this chapter, is about how we are adjusting the sails by extending responsibility, ownership and pride to the people in our corporate setting. About two thirds of our firm's people are members of Generation X. We rely on this group to do most of our work. This is true for most CPA firms and for many other professional service firms.

The question of how to motivate this workforce and the mystery of what makes these younger people tick are topics at many firms'

partner meetings. Much criticism is leveled at Generation Xers' seeming unwillingness to work as hard as their bosses did.

Frequent questions and comments--essentially expressions of frustration punctuated with a question mark at the end--come up as traditional managers and partners wrestle with the changing work-force.

> ***These people are <u>weird</u>. How do we get these people to work as hard as we did? How do these people think we can work forty hour weeks and maintain our current salary levels? Do our younger people want to work as hard as our clients demand of their public accountants?***

Much, if not all, of this criticism is unfair. At our firm we do not deal with many of the frustrations that our colleagues in other firms seem to encounter. Why is this? The answer is fairly simple. The level of frustration by most firms is exacerbated by the use of traditional stimuli to motivate the workforce.

Most firms still believe their workforce is motivated by money and security. Therefore, compensation systems and benefit packages revolve around these presumed motivators.

Fear of losing either money or security does not motivate Generation Xers to work harder.

Quite frankly, they have chosen not to participate in this fear-driven game.

The traditional stimuli simply does not work, yet many Boomers and older managers insist on using fear to motivate their people.

Others develop performance driven bonus systems and sales incentives and then wonder why these fail to achieve desired results. Although the reasons for failure are varied, these techniques are often viewed by the emerging workforce as bribery and are resented.

Our firm's experience from the late eighties through early nineties was that many younger associates did not have the same desires their bosses had at a younger age--including the six figure salary. Complicating this was their belief that the future of public accounting did not seem very bright. Profit trends in our profession were not too promising and liability concerns of partnership had become significant. In the Big Six firms, eligible managers were beginning to refuse the offer of partnership. Others left within a year or two of entering the partnership. As recently as seven or eight years ago these situations rarely, if ever, occurred.

What Generation Xers want is respect, challenge and recognition.

A number of recent surveys by national news magazines show how security and money rank as low as ninth and eleventh in terms of what the emerging workforce desires from an employer. The top three items are:

(1) respect for the individual;
(2) interesting, challenging work with meaningful participation;
(3) recognition of their efforts.

Of these three items, we have the most difficulty with recognition. We keep reminding ourselves to, "Be generous with recognition. If you can't find something to recognize daily, it means you don't know how to look." However, we have a long way to go before we are really generous with recognition or feedback. The concepts discussed in this book focus on creating an environment that encourages and contributes to the top three items, while recognizing the importance of maintaining a certain standard of living and offering a degree of security.

Instead of our shareholder group spending time determining ways to motivate our younger associates, we experience something entirely different. These young people are highly energized and willing to contribute to numerous team efforts. The innovation and creativity offered by this group are largely responsible for the strides our firm is making. The emerging workforce appreciates the opportunity to participate in a variety of projects supported by leadership, and prefer this mode of operation to authoritarian management. They thrive on being an integral part of the firm and appreciate the access to information offered by open book management. This kind of participation may enable the younger associates to develop meaningful relationships many did not experience in childhoods characterized by failed marriages, broken homes and broken promises. Perhaps this involvement can restore some of the trust this generation has not always known.

Personal responsibility is a by-product of the new work ethic.

Another by-product of participation may be the restoration of personal responsibility for one's own actions, a quality that seems to have disappeared during the past twenty or thirty years.

Our younger people bring an understanding of technologies to our firm that is unmatched by other generations. Their desire for a more balanced quality of life is something to be admired and supported, not discouraged. Their unwillingness to wait for much of anything can become a strength, rather than a liability--as most managers and parents now believe. This value has been encouraged by the technological and subsequent consumer revolutions which brought us almost everything quickly and cost effectively.

Young people should prepare to live to be 100.

Given increased life expectancies since the turn of the century many members of this generation will live beyond 100. The changing demographics of our society suggest that they will also work beyond the retirement ages we now know.

- **In the 1950s, seventeen workers supported each retiree.**
- **By 1992, three workers supported each retiree.**
- **By the turn of the century fewer than three workers will support each retiree.**

How the remaining workers will continue to support an aging population remains in question. However, it is certain that people will work years beyond what was once thought possible.

Along with the increased number of working years will be a rate of change previously unknown--driven by technology and shortened product cycles. These factors will force people into multiple careers during a lifetime--as many as five or six unrelated careers. Lifelong learning will become the norm, supported by "learning organizations."

Such lifelong learning will enable people to have self-directed careers to a greater extent than ever before.

We are emphasizing the importance of lifelong learning and self-directed careers to prepare the emerging workforce for successfully adapting to the changes to come. I do not believe Generation X will resist these changes. Instead, they will embrace them.

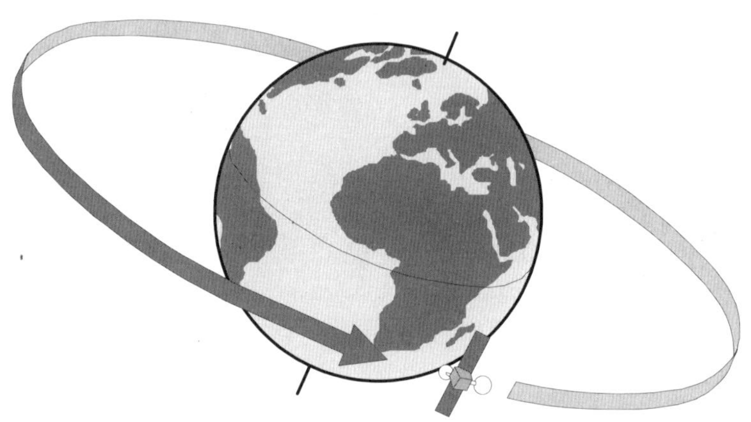

New work habits for a radically changing world.

Recently, I ordered copies so everyone in our firm would have the opportunity to read Price Pritchett's book, *The Employee Handbook of New Work Habits for a Radically Changing World.* In the book, he discusses the thirteen rules for job success in the information age:

- **Become a quick-change artist.**
- **Commit fully to your job.**
- **Speed up.**
- **Accept ambiguity and uncertainty.**
- **Behave like you're in business for yourself.**
- **Stay in school.**
- **Hold yourself accountable for outcomes.**
- **Add value.**

- **See yourself as a service center.**
- **Manage your own morale.**
- **Practice *kaizen (continual improvement).***
- **Be a fixer, not a finger-pointer.**
- **Alter your expectations.**

None of the thirteen rules resemble the handbook I attempted to follow for most of my career. Those rules served the industrial age well. However, they will not remain applicable much longer. We are in the midst of the transition to an information age and the rules are changing. In fifty-one pages, Pritchett captures the essence of how individuals must position themselves to profit from these changes. I wish everyone in our firm had read this book in 1994 when it was written. Better late than never!

The book describes the attitudes the workforce of the information age must embrace to maximize its potential. Of the three generations in our present workforce, I believe the Xers will adapt most easily to the new attitudes and skill sets. I am sure that members of this generation who refuse to adapt will fall far short of their potential.

In summary, most of our profession seems to be preoccupied with a concern that their firms cannot attract or retain the level of talent that they once enjoyed. Many firms complain that the people they hire are weird. Changing demographics indicate that this situation will only worsen in the future because the number of accounting graduates is decreasing. These are recurring themes at practice management conferences and partner meetings. In general, I do not doubt that these trends are occurring throughout the profession. However, our firm is clearly bucking these trends.

The by-products of our changed culture are better people, lower turnover and higher adaptability for the future.

We are attracting better people than I have known in my twenty years of public accounting and our turnover rates are lower than I have ever seen. I do not believe this is happening by coincidence, but is a by-product of our changed culture.

Furthermore, I do not share many of my colleagues' concerns about the emerging work force. I believe the only people who should be concerned are those who work for organizations that continue to believe that if given enough seasoning, Generation X will come around to their way of thinking. As these organizations become more dependent on the emerging workforce, they need to change their model.

The old formulas and contracts simply do not work.

Organizations that fail to recognize these changes will probably die before the Xers convert to the old ways.

Chapter 6. Affecting Change Through Process Teams

♦ Focusing too tightly on problems blinded us to creative innovations ♦ False gods: Crisis-driven thinking ♦ Work harder, not smarter ♦ Evolution and adaptation into a TQM system that worked, but not instantly ♦ Process Teams were not just lingo; they became integral to our working experience ♦ Outside help enabled us to learn how to work in teams successfully ♦ "Six Phases of a Project" ♦ Some early projects of the process teams

In 1991, we were a crisis managed accounting firm driven by deadlines. Often, we barely met the external deadlines and rarely met the internal ones.

This was evident in our daily mental framework. We were results driven and desired control of outcomes. We were quick to fix blame, to determine who or what was wrong. We were unwilling to admit that our processes and cultures kept our people from achieving excellence or sometimes even from performing their jobs. We kept waiting for the day we finally had the right mix of people. As mentioned earlier, we were fear driven--fear of losing a client, fear of failure in the eyes of management, fear of financial failure. We were quick to analyze and build databases and slow to take any action. We never quite had enough information to finalize decisions and almost always overstated the financial constraints. We focused on fixing problems--not on innovating.

Focusing too tightly on problems blinded us to creative innovations

This described our firm's attitude in 1991.

Often we encouraged false economies. We "got by" with old broken down computers and an insufficient number of printers that were held together with duct tape and paper clips. We were slow to upgrade the fleet of 286's and 386s because they were fast enough for the DOS applications we used. We believed accounting firms would not need any computer faster than these because we only used spreadsheets and word processing.

We had one 486 that was capable of running Windows word processing. This computer was saved for proposals. Since no one knew enough about Windows, we manually cut and pasted page numbers, graphics, etc. Any accountant who used a mouse was a sissy. Real accountants used DOS. We failed to realize the power of these electronic tools and as a result were asking our people to build skyscrapers with hand tools.

Another item we overlooked was the time wasted by our people while waiting for the slow machines to perform. Worse, we underestimated the negative impact of the annual busy season printer range wars on our operations. We not only had to stop the fighting, but we also had to finance the peace!

Our thoughts and actions--or lack thereof--focused on the almighty dollar. We believed if we were frugal enough we could pay our people well. Given this commitment, everyone would work harder to get the job done.

False gods--Crisis driven thinking; Work harder, not smarter.

There were two problems with this line of thinking. First, it was still crisis driven thinking. We expected people to work harder, not smarter. Second, we set ourselves up for failure by putting far too much emphasis on compensation. Like most managers of the era, we were foolish enough to believe people worked for money. Sure, they work for two paychecks each month, but they work better when they feel useful--when they are contributing and having an impact on the organization. When they are involved they begin to work with the kind of resourcefulness, willingness and innovative power required of everyone in the organization to achieve the fundamental purpose, or vision, of the organization.

By 1991, many Total Quality Management efforts were beginning to fail, so we were afraid to call our efforts TQM. We attributed most of these failures to the inability of U.S. management to understand or accept the fundamental changes Dr. Deming's philosophies required.

Most corporate efforts underestimated the difficulty of forcing systemic change and the training required at all levels of the company. Also, many managers viewed TQM as the latest corporate fad which would soon go the way of Management by Objectives and a myriad of others that had come and gone. As a result, they were not committed to the concepts and many saw TQM as an opportunity to push some of the problems to the line workers in quality circles. Soon the workers would see how difficult it was to fix things and everyone would return to the old ways of doing things.

Evolution and adaptation into a TQM system that worked, but not instantly.

So how did we approach it differently? How did we bring a group of crisis driven, left-brained accountants into a new working system that employed many of Dr. Deming's Total Quality Management principles? Without going through all the twists and turns of our evolution into TQM, here are the basics of how we started and some examples of what we experienced as a result of the many changes we instituted. But, be forewarned: ***We did not always have immediate success.*** For example, we started by changing the names of several parts of our business. The audit department became the *audit team*, the tax department became the *tax team* and the management committee became the *sales team*. We paid lip service to this for six months--thinking we were really taking a giant leap into TQM. What happened? Nothing, which should not surprise you. What did we get out of this? Crisis driven management--same thing as in the past. It took us six months to realize it.

However, in the process we were discovering that we needed to reengineer our internal system entirely in order to improve our ability to provide quality services, and ultimately, to increase our profits. So we began to focus on internal quality and process improvement.

Process Teams were not just lingo; they became integral to our working experience.

In late 1993, we formed four process teams:

(1) **The Common Area Team's** responsibility was to improve the processes in the reception area, library, conference room, file room, kitchen and hallways.

(2) **The Technology Team** made the technology decisions in the office. These included computers, software, the network, voice mail, e-mail, fax, copy machines, etc. Later, scanning equipment, CD Rom, remote processing and the Internet became the team's responsibility.

(3) **The Client Services Team** began the cultural change from a product driven firm to a client relationship driven firm. This team also focused on improving our processes related to client service. They reviewed the cycle from the time a prospect called; to the time

we delivered a proposal; to the time we were hired; to the time we planned, executed and delivered our work product; to the time we billed and collected for our services; and finally to the time we were rehired to do the next project.

(4) **The Human Resources Team** handled fringe benefits, the evaluation and counseling system, firm social events, the bonus and compensation systems, and continuing professional education.

We explained that anyone could participate on any or all teams and participation was totally voluntary. People did not have to participate on a process team. However, working toward and striving for quality was a job requirement.

What we learned during the next year is that our people did not know how to operate in teams. We thought we had empowered people to participate actively on teams, but something entirely different happened. When the teams gathered, a committee mentality prevailed.

Most of the team members played things very close to the vest until they had an idea of what the senior ranking person present really wanted to do. This did not exactly result in innovative thinking or team dynamics. Teams, unsure of the limits of their authority, generally underestimated them. As a result, the teams were not effective and by the end of the first year of their existence they rarely if ever met.

We did not know how to think in terms of processes. What a paradox for a group of accountants who had spent years working in and around accounting systems! However, it was true.

Outside help enabled us to learn how to work in teams successfully.

During 1994, Karl Krumm was charged with the responsibility of teaching us to work in teams and think in processes. In that regard, we were successful. One of the most important actions was to authorize each process team to spend up to $500 to improve any process that advanced client service or enhanced our people's working conditions. Spending decisions greater than $500 were to be presented to the Noname Team by the respective process team leader. With this guidance, the teams knew the parameters of their authority. The teams began to function as I had envisioned.

They began to appreciate the reality of being actively involved in various projects--that active team involvement on complicated projects is not all wine and roses. All of the team leaders and most team members could write chapters about the truth and wisdom embodied in the following articulation of these important ideas.

"Six Phases of a Project"

Enthusiasm
Disillusionment
Panic
Search for the Guilty
Punishment of the Innocent
Praise & Honors for the Non-Participants

--Anonymous

The next several pages describe a few of the early experiences of the process teams. Some of the stories may seem a bit trivial, but their purpose is to reinforce the truths that "people will be people" and progress will be slow. Some of our early experiences caused us to pause and reflect. Our organization was tempted from time to time to return to the traditional management approach. I have had to resist this temptation at least every two or three months of our journey.

When determining initial project assignments, we had to crawl before we could walk, walk before we could jog, and jog before we could run.

Our few early successes were important, especially during the times we were bandaging skinned knees and setting broken bones! Setbacks are the reality of implementing this part of the cultural revolution, but should not scare anyone from attempting the change. In hindsight, some of the bumps we encountered along the way were an important part of growing up. Some of the seemingly trivial moments provided the most important learning experiences. All of these experiences, good and bad, paved the way for where we are today.

Our current status may be best compared to a jogger who is training to increase his speed by two minutes a mile, while increasing his distance from a 10K to a half marathon. We expect to accomplish this during the next four months.

Some early projects of the process teams:

Common Areas

Common Area Team--Common areas included the reception area, the conference room, the kitchen, the file room, the library and hallways. We had some real problems keeping these areas clean and organized. Dishes never got put in the dishwasher. A sign hung over the kitchen sink that said, "Your mother doesn't work here."

This sign was about as effective as your December diet and the subsequent New Year's resolution. The library table was frequently stacked with open research books no one bothered to return to the book shelves. The next person would come in and open their books right on top of the ones already lying there, then leave those as well.

Every two weeks an outside librarian would come in and clean up the mess. Our conference room chairs had buttons that were regressed about two inches in the seats and backs. People would bet on how full the holes would become with crumbs and popcorn before someone would turn the chair over and dump the collection.

Examples like these are not at all uncommon in corporate America. They demonstrate at least two serious weaknesses in our traditional culture--a general lack of ownership in the workplace and the attitude that the more menial tasks are always someone else's job. People think they are too important to return their cups to the dishwasher, re-file documents or vacuum chairs.

Initially, I believed by constantly reinforcing the reality that we did not hire maids, people would get the message it was everyone's responsibility to maintain a clean work environment. Next, I tried setting an example by loading the dishwasher, filing books, vacuuming chairs and polishing furniture after hours. This had just the opposite effect I desired.

People assumed I had become the shareholder in charge of cleaning common areas. Soon, an even greater number of coffee cups appeared in the sink. Worse, we fought the kitchen war of 1992 where the sign mentioned above became an anonymous memo signed by "The Management." This situation then deteriorated into a series of points and counterpoints on the bottom of the memo. I do not remember how the war ended, but the process made no one happy.

The job of the Common Area Team was to observe the common areas and make recommendations to the entire office to keep the office more presentable. The team soon became the "Tomcat Team" because it was led by Tom Locke.

This team took its job ***seriously***.

At first, the Common Area Team's actions were subtle.

A team member would quietly remove a cup from the sink and place it in the dishwasher. Another would return library books to the bookshelf. Then the team got really bold and someone actually purchased a vacuum cleaner for the office so we could clean the conference room chairs. Slowly the rest of the office would come around, but it was not happening fast enough for the team.

We began to hear comments such as, "We need to get that library cleaned up." Whoever happened to be around at the time became a part of the clean up crew. Anyone who walked by during the activity ended up spending the entire day purging the library of outdated or duplicated books. One crew carried five trash barrels (big ones) full of old stuff to the dumpster. When they finished an entire wall of the library was empty.

The kitchen became cleaner, too. It seems the Tomcats, now also known as the housekeeping police, had managed to show everyone in the office the location of the dishwasher, *which had never moved.* Throughout the office, pride in the appearance of the common areas was beginning to take hold.

Cleaning and organizing these common areas did not happen without incident.

There was a major disagreement when the team decided to rearrange the file room. They cleaned and organized supplies and replaced unused cabinets with more suitable storage. All agreed these were positive changes, but when they moved the postage meter to allow more space in the report binding area, they made their first mistake. And it was a big one. No one denied the binding area was too cramped. However, the team failed to ask the one person in the office who used the postage meter what she thought would work best.

Words cannot describe the morning after the evening the postage meter was moved three feet. We did not have a storm--we had a major hurricane. By ten the next morning, there were coalitions forming of those who supported returning the meter to its original location and those who liked the new location. By noon, people were no longer speaking to each other and hostile notes were being traded via mail boxes. Thank goodness we didn't have e-mail back then.

Fortunately, by the end of the day, the team leader stepped in, forced a team meeting, and invited the operator of the postage meter to attend. The result was total rearrangement of the room itself into a much more efficient work area.

Where did the postage meter end up? Completely across the room.

The moral of the story is: Never move a machine without consulting the operator.

Dr. Deming would have told us that. In the final analysis, we learned a great deal about teamwork. On a positive note, changes were made to the file room during a twenty-four hour period that would have taken years under the old system.

The team also worked on reducing the time visitors spent in our waiting room and improving the manner in which our phones were answered (including options to enter voice mail).

Since everyone served their own coffee, the kitchen became one of the first stops for our visitors. This reinforced the need for the kitchen to be presentable. The nasty kitchen signs were replaced with Dilbert cartoons that generally made fun of most of our reengineering efforts.

In particular, they made fun of me. Once I would have been offended. Now I actually welcomed this interaction.

Our dinosaur-library was captured on CD ROM.

With the dynamic changes that had occurred as a result of the technology team's efforts in 1994, we no longer needed a large space for our library. Our entire library was converted to CD ROM which freed up a considerable amount of space. The library, located immediately behind the reception area, had become an embarrassment. We realized that visiting college students saw it as something between a museum piece and a dinosaur.

In redesigning this space, we were able to expand the reception room to allow for the consolidation of our scattered support staff. The team believed our redesigned space would increase the efficiency of our administrative personnel and provide built-in relief for the receptionist, who had been stationed in a separate island reception area. The renovation called for the removal of several walls to create the large open space, and originally I was not convinced of the new design. Fortunately, however, I deferred to the judgment of the team.

The redesigned area yields many benefits.

After a year in this redesigned space, several by-products of the team's efforts have become apparent. First, the introduction of natural light to this area has been revitalizing. Next, the central support area has become a gathering place for our people. And since it opens to the reception area, any client waiting for two or three minutes, our benchmark, is likely to see several of our people. Under the former design, clients waiting in our reception area saw our receptionist, the person they came to see and anyone who breezed by on their way to the rest room. The latter were never really in much of a mood to visit. As a result of the new open concept, I am sure many of our people met more tax clients this past busy season than in the previous five years combined. I know I did.

Technology

Technology Team--The Technology Team is probably our greatest success story. As recently as 1994, our office was running on computers that would make the IRS cringe. We had one 486 with Windows capability. We had three 386s and a handful of those old suitcase style 286s that our auditors had to haul around and fight over in the field. Tax professionals complained there were never computers or printers available from February through April because auditors were in house taking up valuable computer time.

Auditors were embarrassed at what they were having to lug to client locations. In short, the hardware situation was a *disaster* and the software circumstances were even *worse.* Management knew we had problems and we tried very hard to schedule computers and computer time to accommodate as many people as possible. This system was not working well and the ensuing arguments over computer time were often heated. It got so bad that some of our tax professionals started offering to buy their own 486s and bring them to the office.

Everyone's perception was we did not have the money to upgrade.

In walks the Technology Team. If you polled the people in our firm, you would be told our greatest changes have been made by the Technology Team. This team was presented with probably the most challenging, and most necessary, task of any team. They were asked to put together a plan to update our entire computer system.

For several years, the network had grown like an amoeba. Our software was hodgepodge and our hardware was worse than poor. Numerous operating systems were used and everyone loaded our machines with their own favorite spreadsheets, data bases and word processing programs. Worse, very few user manuals were available in the office and toll free software support numbers were a luxury of the past.

The Technology Team was faced with a huge challenge.

In August 1994, the team decided to hire a consultant to help them. This was actually a rather novel idea for our firm. After all, why would a bunch of accountants need outside help with their own accounting and operating system? We found out.

The consultant did a preliminary study and refused to work with us until we trashed the old system and purchased a new one.

He knew better than to put any more patches on our antiquated mess. He told us it was impossible to continue with the old "fix it to get by" mentality which was born of budget constraints. In the past we would ask, "What can we afford?" Now the team comes to the management group and says, "This is what we need. How do we buy it?"

Within three months, the Technology Team trashed all 286s and most 386s and purchased enough 486s so every professional had either a desk top or a notebook at their disposal. The number of printers in the office tripled. The network was new, our software was integrated and every member of the firm was required to attend at least two days of training on the new system.

All old files were converted to the updated software, and our library was converted from books to CD ROM. We converted to Windows and acquired a suite package of software.

Everyone had forty-five days to convert their files to the new system, or lose them. Many people in the office believed this demand was unreasonable and impossible; however, we accomplished the Technology Team's goal.

Over the next year the results were amazing. Everyone learned to use Windows and the new system at the same time and at different paces. As a group we benefitted because there was always someone within earshot who had already overcome the barrier another person had just encountered. We began seeing our computers as more than high tech calculators and typewriters. ***Even the shareholders learned.*** We began doing most of our own correspondence and spreadsheets. I will not elaborate on the wonder of this miracle, especially on my part.

In the field, auditors began preparing audit reports on site. Report drafts were reviewed with clients prior to our last day of field work. This beat our old timetable by somewhere between two and six weeks. By 1996, three administrative people supported the efforts of thirty accountants. Many firms our size have a support staff more than twice as large as ours.

Why is this story so amazing?

The strategic decision to invest in technology was made in August and implemented within ninety days. The shareholders participated only in the strategic decision which was predicated on our desire to become a Windows environment and to buy a suite package of software. They approved the capital expenditure of $80,000.

We assigned the implementation of an $80,000 project to a team led by a 26 year-old tax specialist. No member of management was on this team. Only a year earlier, the decision to buy one computer took weeks or months. The shareholders would *never* have considered handing $80,000 to a team of inexperienced people. Even if we had, we would have managed the project every step of the way--in spite of being clueless about the technology being discussed. This time we left them alone! We had come a long way. We could not have handed the project to a better group of people.

Within ninety days, the project was successfully implemented.

The technology team has done a tremendous job of improving the efficiency and effectiveness of our people. Talk about direct implementation of our mission statement! This has been it--providing a quality environment so our people could effectively produce a quality product. With the improved technology, every individual in the firm became more creative and more client service oriented. Why? Simply because we had time to move our focus from number crunching to business consulting. It was no longer solely the responsibility of management to notice areas for improvement and address them with the clients.

Now, every member of our firm is challenged to be solutions driven and every member of our firm meets the challenge. More importantly, our people have been empowered to do so. We allow individuals to review a client's situation and determine for themselves if they are qualified to address it. This is far removed from the old days when every issue, every correspondence, every minor matter had to be relayed to management for consideration before action benefiting the client could be taken. This is a ***revolutionary*** move for an accounting firm--and it is working.

Client Services

Client Services Team--The Client Services Team was charged with the task of polling our current clients, to discover what types of services they felt they were getting and what services they would like to receive. Once the information was gathered, the team established or refined processes to allow us to better meet the needs of our clients.

The team determined our failure was not on the individual audit and tax services provided, but in the internal cross-communication between the departments. As a result, we restructured the client service process. Cross-discipline teams were established to service each client. This allowed for better communication between the audit team and the tax team, as well as increasing our ability to consult with clients in a timely manner.

The proof was in the feedback from clients.

What kind of feedback have we received on this service improvement? One client told us he had never received this quality service from any accounting firm. He said, "I don't know what your group changed over there, but it is working. Keep it up!" What else? In 1994, we proudly received the Quality Vendor of the Year Award from Austin White Lime Company, a highly respected Austin establishment for over 100 years. This was significant to me because in my years of public accounting, this was the first time I had seen an accounting firm receive such a formal recognition for service excellence.

Another reason for its significance was the plaque that the company presented to us and the words inscribed upon it:

"Quality is never an accident; it is always the result of high intention, sincere effort, intelligent direction and skillful execution; it represents the wise choice of many alternatives."

These are the same words on the plaque we purchased in 1991 for display in our conference room. We put this special award in our conference room and moved the original plaque to our reception area.

By 1994, the team's name and function became the Client Service-Marketing Team. This change reflected our belief that client service and marketing are one and the same. It also demonstrated our belief that the vast majority of our marketing potential rested within our existing client base. First we had to focus on delivering quality services to our existing clients, to at least meet and hopefully exceed their expectations.

Many firms concentrate so much on developing new clients that they ignore serving those they already have. This approach can prove costly, even if the marketing program is an apparent success.

When we accomplished quality service delivery, we could emphasize offering additional services to existing clients and seeking referrals from satisfied clients.

Client appreciation event.

With this philosophy in mind, the team organized our first client appreciation event. We leased the local theater for an evening and hosted a reception and private performance for our clients, our friends (referral sources) and our own people. Over two hundred people attended. Not only did everyone enjoy the evening, but the event was also a tremendous outreach tool for the theater. We hit a client relations home run. The team improved on the second annual event and has committed to making this a centerpiece of our client appreciation efforts.

The new client package.

The team developed what became known as the "new client package." Included in the package is an in-house publication, "Our Clients, Our People," which describes services offered, clients and industries served, a history and description of our firm and resumes of the Client Services Team.

For two years we had worked on and debated the merits of a firm brochure. Finally, we decided against a slick brochure, thinking instead that we had done pretty well for the last four years without a brochure. Also, it occurred to us that our firm was changing too quickly for us to finalize one.

The team decided to leave the firm's biography, entitled "Our Clients, Our People," on the word processor, where changes could be made quickly and inexpensively. Also included in the new client package are a letter welcoming the new client to our firm, an engagement letter, recent newsletters, tax planning booklets, business cards, a listing of direct phone lines, a map to our office and parking directions.

Dilemmas solved with the new client package.

The ***new client package*** also provided the answer to the disjointed process of establishing a new client in our internal systems. Unbelievable as it may seem, this process used to be pretty haphazard! No such package existed. Whatever the new client asked for and received in the proposal process was all the information about our firm they received. Although we generally did a good job of selling our firm during the proposal process, our marketing efforts went downhill from the moment we were hired.

This is difficult to admit, but generally true. When we answered the phone call that communicated our selection, we thanked the new client and told them we would send an engagement letter. Later, someone established an account number for the new client in our billing system. This usually happened when the first person attempting to charge time to the client found that no number existed. Within a couple of months a newsletter was mailed and the new client was added to the mailing list. Hopefully, someone in the tax department established the client on the due date monitoring list. The first time someone needed to call the client, the phone number was added to our phone list. Often, adding a new client to all the necessary systems took several weeks or months.

As the new client package was developed, the Client Services-Marketing Team decided it would become the catalyst for collecting all the necessary information. Along with the new client package, the team developed a form that included all the necessary information for our internal systems. Several independent processes became one.

It was a powerful affirmation that our people were beginning to think of everything as an ***interconnected*** process. The use of the new client package soon expanded to prospects, recruits, career days and other interested parties. Prototype letters were developed for each situation. We even used the package to communicate a recent combination with another accounting firm. In 1995, the team designed coffee cups with our firm logo. These were sent with new client packages and to our existing clients with audit reports and tax returns. This was a simple thing to do, but we were surprised by how much positive feedback we received from clients.

Introduction of the Atomic Model

The team recently decided to begin changing the marketing culture of our firm through a redefined approach to delivering services called the ***Atomic Model.*** This model requires our people to assume the role of becoming the ***preferred business advisors*** to our clients. The model also requires many people to assume the role of rainmakers--instead of rainmaking being confined to the more experienced people in the firm. Currently, many of our clients identify us as their auditors or tax accountants who are occasionally called upon to provide advice or perform a special project.

This is a significant cultural change and requires a serious investment in training. The team developed appropriate training that was conducted during the next several months. The Atomic Model and marketing training are discussed in Chapters 12 and 13.

Human Resources

Human Resources Team--The Human Resources Team was asked to review our personnel policies, evaluations, fringe benefits, and compensation policies.

And that was a job!

The team took responsibility for making health insurance decisions (a thankless task), planning office parties and picnics, reviewing professional memberships and overseeing continuing professional education. Efforts of this team even included establishing a cafeteria plan. This would save tax dollars for both the employee and the firm. Within four weeks the team had investigated and implemented a plan and we were signing people up.

Establishment of the cafeteria plan saved members of our firm over $20,000 in its first year!

Powerful changes occurred in evaluation and personnel policies.

The Human Resources Team replaced the firm's evaluation and counseling systems with a new system of frequent, informal feedback sessions supported by cross functional mentoring teams. The team replaced the performance driven bonus system with an office wide profit sharing system. Chapter 11 is devoted to the profit sharing system developed by this team.

In 1995, the team significantly revised our firm's dated personnel manual to reflect the current policies of the firm. Within sixty days the team had revised the manual to reflect the numerous changes that had evolved over the past five years, but had gone unrecorded. An important aspect of this project was management's commitment to delegate the rewrite effort to the Human Resources Team. Unlike previous revisions, which had taken hours of shareholder time, only one shareholder participated in the process, and then only as a regular team member. The shareholders had enough confidence in the team concept to say "just do it." Recently, the team liquidated our former 401(k) and established a new and improved plan. Also, the team offered the office a new concept of self-directed continuing education that replaced the management-directed system. Currently, the team is analyzing the results of an officewide survey that covers most aspects of our work environment and reengineering efforts.

The Human Resources Team's efforts have demonstrated an ability to respond to suggestions in a timely and efficient manner. In the past we proudly said that our people were our most important asset. However, our actions rarely supported this proclamation. Continuing education, fringe benefits, personnel evaluations and personnel manuals were largely ignored until a deadline approached or a crisis occurred. Even social events were planned and executed at the last minute. It was almost impossible to get anyone to devote any attention to these matters. Often a manager or partner reluctantly assumed these responsibilities.

The efforts of the Human Resources Team have changed the traditional paradigm that resulted in personnel matters being largely ignored.

Now, a dynamic cross-functional group of people regularly responds to the human resource needs of our people. The positive results are significant. Our human resource systems are continually improved, as are our attitudes and the other tools we need to better serve our clients.

Chapter 7. Challenges of the Evolving Leadership Team

◆ The team went through five names in five years ◆ The purpose of our leadership meetings had been to disseminate information to the troops ◆ By 1994, we were beginning to learn more about the dynamics of teams ◆ By 1995, a fundamental governance issue was becoming apparent ◆ In mid 1995, we aggressively shook and forever changed the governance of the firm ◆ A series of emotional discussions ensued and some feelings were hurt ◆ In summary, coordination of efforts of process teams has greatly improved

---

One of the more amusing aspects of our reengineering effort has been the evolution of the leadership team. Tracking the evolution can best be done by following its ever-changing name:

In 1991, it was the Management Committee.

In 1992, the Sales Team.

In early 1994, the Strategic Implementation Team.

In late 1994, it became the Strategic Success Team.

And in 1995 through 1997--the **Noname** Team. Regardless of how it looks, though, the firm's leadership did not go from total control to total anonymity, which may have resulted in anarchy!

We wanted a leadership system which differed from the monthly partner-manager meetings of our previous Big Six firm.

In the past, our partner-manager meetings were venues for management to disseminate information.

Generally, it was not an appropriate forum for discussion or decision making. We decided to emulate some of the law firms who effectively administered their practices through a Management Committee.

Initially, we expected our partners and managers (now called *shareholders* and *senior associates*--another emulation of the law firms) to serve on the Management Committee. However, we recognized that over a period of time not everyone would have an interest in participating in the management of the firm, nor would we expect this of everyone. In the early days of the firm, we definitely moved toward team decision making, but we still called ourselves a committee. Also, the degree to which we began to rely on the group to make decisions required us to meet every two weeks.

After about a year of this system, a couple of developments occurred. The "management" in the committee's name seemed to encourage a division between management and staff. I have never quite understood this phenomenon.

Discussion around the office began to sound like a union environment, but the terminology changed. Now everything seemed to be discussed in terms of "Management versus Staff." Another situation revolved around the use of the word "Committee." Every decision seemed to be referred to the Management Committee--sometimes with the hope and belief it would be lost and never resurface. Often, this was the case.

Some hoped for Divine Intervention.

By early 1992, we were near bankruptcy in an environment that resembled a collective bargaining arrangement. On the bright side, the administrative issues that the Management Committee had spent considerable time addressing in the early months, were taking fewer hours.

After giving this circumstance thought, we changed the name of the Management Committee to the Sales Team. The idea was intended to focus our leadership efforts on selling our way out of financial problems. We also hoped the name change would move us away from the "Management versus Staff" conflict.

By 1994, we were beginning to learn more about the dynamics of teams.

At the very least we had started using several of the correct buzz words. I began to think about the benefits of aligning the name of the Sales Team to more closely reflect what it had become. It had clearly evolved into a form of "think tank" for the establishment and implementation of the firm's strategic directives. By the end of my thought process, the Sales Team had become The Strategic Implementation Team. Although some people seemed to like this change, within weeks we became known as the SIT Team. This acronym was not exactly what I had in mind. People would pass the conference room with glass doors and comment that the SIT Team was at it again and looked pretty comfortable.

It took a little more time before I came up with a name, Strategic Success Team, that also had an acronym "SST" to fit the desired dynamics. Leaders have to do something with all their time! This name served our leadership team well, and at least by now we could joke about it.

By 1995, a fundamental governance issue was becoming apparent.

The Strategic Success Team had grown to ten senior associates and shareholders and it was apparent not everyone had an interest in participating in the periodic meetings. However, most people were reluctant to state this. After all, conventional wisdom thought the title "management" was a right of passage and managers were expected to attend management meetings.

An even larger fundamental issue was that our process teams had become so successful, they were effectively running the office. However, the team leaders did not have a forum for coordinating their efforts, and only one of the four team leaders was on the Strategic Success Team.

The more effective the process teams became, the more interrelated they became. As a result the process teams worked in vacuums and the team leaders felt detached and isolated. Worse--members of the Strategic Success Team, individually and collectively, were frequently sticking their noses into team matters and messing things up.

I was guilty, too. Sometimes I cannot resist getting involved before I am asked. I think that goes with being an ENTJ in the Myers-Briggs scheme of things. The ENTJ personality traits include extroverted habits, ability to organize, need to control, ability to analyze and propensity to think ahead. Most CEOs are tested as ENTJs. I am trying to overcome some of the negatives inherent in my personality traits, but it is hard to "change the spots on a leopard."

In mid 1995, we aggressively shook and forever changed the governance of the firm.

We formed a new leadership team, comprised of four shareholders, four process team leaders and the team leader of a special task force.

The team leaders were two traditional managers, a part time associate, a twenty-six year old associate and a secretary. The leadership team was comprised of five men and four women. All members would be exposed to and actively participate in establishing and implementing virtually all of the firm's strategies. The team, which is effectively the firm's *board of directors*, is cross functional, ranges in age from twenty-six to fifty-nine, is almost gender balanced, and includes part time representation. The diversity offered by our governance may not be the only of its kind, but there are not many like it.

Once again, we had discussions about what to call this newly constructed leadership team.

We even had an office wide contest to name the team. Weeks passed. The team began to take shape. Still, we had no suitable entries in the contest.

Finally, we borrowed a name from Indian Guides of the YMCA. Each fall new tribes are introduced to the federation. Deciding on a name for the tribe is usually not accomplished before the first camp out. At the first federation campfire, these unnamed tribes are introduced as the **Noname** Tribe (The "Indian" pronunciation is NO-NAH-MEE). In the ML&R tradition of borrowing and improving good ideas from others, our leadership team became the Noname Team. I believe the name will stick because it seems to fit most situations. The biggest shortcoming to the name is people outside our office have difficulty understanding the relevance of the Noname name. However, it has become a very useful conversation piece and has effectively conveyed a lighter side to our generally serious business. So much for the team name.

An indication of the extent to which the Noname Team is responsible for strategic decisions is the frequency of shareholder meetings. During the past year the shareholders have met as a group to discuss office operations on only three occasions. Topics that required these meetings included the only secrets that remain with the shareholders' group--raises, confidential recruiting decisions, negotiations to acquire another practice and sensitive client matters.

What have the *results* of the reconstituted leadership team been? Several months after the creation of the Noname Team, we had an uncomfortable experience. After the Human Resources Team had spent many hours on a significant project, a progress report was made to the Noname Team. During the discussion it became apparent the team had expanded its original mission beyond the understanding of several Noname Team members, including me. These Noname Team members were concerned that the new direction would result in significantly more project time than originally discussed and would possibly jeopardize an important client referral source.

A series of emotional discussions ensued and some feelings were hurt.

The process team felt betrayed and believed the rug had been pulled out from under its feet; however, in the final analysis the Noname system functioned exactly as intended. In the past, the process team would have worked in a vacuum with damaging results to the overall strategies of the firm. Under the new system, the process team may not have liked the results of the coordination and oversight provided by the Noname Team, but realized the system ultimately worked to the benefit of the firm. The wounds from this type of experience will heal.

In summary, coordination of efforts of process teams has greatly improved.

The change has effectively communicated that in the new ML&R, management is no longer a rite of passage. Management of the firm has been replaced by the concept of *leadership*, which crosses gender lines, age groups, experience levels, career tracks and functions. Finally, the Noname Team has become the free flowing think tank we only hoped possible before we found the right formula.

The team meets every other week for one and a half hours. The agenda includes opening remarks by the leading shareholders, status reports from each process team leader, and then other matters, as appropriate. The variety of perspectives on any particular issue is remarkable. A typical discussion might begin with the perspective of a shareholder, be refined by a twenty-six year old, then challenged by a part time associate and refined by a support person's perspective. The group considers these perspectives and makes the final decision. Sometimes the team decides we failed to ask the right question and the process begins again. The dynamics of the team decision-making process are unbelievable. Cross functional team decisions are almost always better than those made by individuals in the past. "Management versus Staff" discussions have disappeared. The traditional battles and sometimes wars between accountants and administrators have disappeared. No longer are 75 percent of management's discussions focused on complaining about the administrators in the office.

Recently we took a step to broaden our outreach and diversity. On a rotational basis, three people who are not regular Noname Team members will join us at each meeting. Also, we have begun a rotational policy for process team leaders. Original process team leaders handed their reins to team members who had taken an active interest in their respective team. The energy required of the team leaders is incredible and exhausting, so we think this move will reduce burnout among team leaders. Another benefit of rotation is having the immediate past team leader available to provide back up and support to the new team leader.

During 1996, four of the original process team leaders transferred their roles to new team leaders. I am interested in other by-products of these moves. I think they will be positive.

Chapter 8. Increasing Profits Through Strategic Alliances

♦ Strategic alliances and core values--**Attitude** ♦ When we introduce ourselves, who do we say we are? ♦ In the past, I introduced myself as a CPA ♦ Then I tried impressing them with how busy I was ♦ Now, it's, "I'm Earl Maxwell, a business advisor trained as a CPA." ♦ How do you get out of the box? ♦ CPAs must begin thinking of and positioning ourselves to be the ***preferred business advisor*** to our clients ♦ CPA firms have become our biggest referral source ♦ Strategic alliances and core values--**Trust** ♦ Two of the Big Six firms refer work to us that does not fit their economic model ♦ Several local firms refer significant work to us ♦ International Strategic Alliances: AFAi ♦ Strategic alliances and core values: **Open communication and flexibility**

The ability of organizations to search for and effectively establish *strategic alliances* is critically important. This is especially true of the vast majority of professional service firms, which in the overall scheme of things tend to be fairly small organizations.

The exceptions, the Big Six accounting and consulting firms, employ between 30,000 and 60,000 people. Although the Big Six are forming strategic alliances, they tend to be linking with other giants in the financial services and technology arenas. These strategic alliances are based on many of the same concepts discussed in this chapter and provide interesting case studies.

However, instead of suggesting emulation of giant strategic alliances, the focus of this chapter will be an examination of ways for the "little guys" to more effectively compete with the "big guys" through strategic alliances.

Since 1991, we have been moving toward strategic alliances--even before we heard the term. During the past five years, we have learned the basic ingredients for successfully forming these alliances.

Strategic alliances and core values--Attitude.

Before our discussion of strategic alliances, we must mention the need for tradition-bound CPAs to begin thinking of ourselves differently. A new attitude is imperative.

What does this mean? ***We have to expand the narrow definition of what we do and what we are willing to do for the benefit of our clients.***

How long will it take? ***Longer than you think.***

How difficult is this? ***About as difficult as giving birth.***

For the past twenty years the accounting profession has stressed the need for specialization, citing as its reason that the world had become too complicated for the generalist. To a certain extent, this was true. However, we probably applied the specialization concept to a greater extent than was healthy--for either the individual service providers or the clients they served.

When we introduce ourselves, who do we say we are?

As we go around the room to introduce ourselves to a new firm member, the introductions focus on whether we are an *audit* specialist or a *tax* specialist. In larger firms, the introductions focus on *functional* or *industry* specialization. If we introduce ourselves to each other in this manner, we must do the same to our clients, friends and the public. No wonder our clients and friends perceive us to be stuck in a very small box, or to have the box over our heads!

Much has been made of stepping out of the box. Advertising campaigns assure us that certain companies will step out of the box for our benefit. Quite frankly, I am tired of hearing about the box and now avoid referring to it. Instead, let's concentrate on thinking of our roles differently and introducing ourselves differently. When we do this, the people to whom we are introduced respond differently.

In the past, I introduced myself as a CPA.

This usually encouraged a question related to taxes--to which I replied I was an auditor and really knew very little about taxes. So much for the conversation. To think I encouraged being put in such a small box by so many people for so many years is unforgivable!

Then I tried impressing them with how busy I was.

Accountants somehow believe this confirms our sense of value and self worth. Unfortunately, those around us see it differently. Some feel sorry we have our priorities so fouled up. Others are not interested. Some of our best friends believe they are doing our families a favor by referring work to another accountant--and do so.

For several years, I have not told anyone how busy I have been. If they begin the conversation with a statement concerning how busy I must be, my reply is, "We have been pretty busy, but we still have room for another good client." I learned this from one of my partners. It is one of his favorite sayings and it seems to be effective.

Now, it's, "I'm Earl Maxwell, a business advisor trained as a CPA."

In an introduction situation that demands a one sentence statement I reply, ***"I am a business advisor trained as a CPA."*** I learned this from Karl Krumm who introduces himself as an organizational consultant trained as a clinical psychologist.

If provided more time to introduce myself, I reply, "My name is Earl Maxwell. I am the father of two boys and have been married to their Mother for twenty-two years. I enjoy family and church activities. My activities in the community focus on education, work force development and health and human service issues. I work for the firm Maxwell Locke & Ritter, and the things I enjoy most are working in the areas of reengineering, strategic planning and business processes."

This different way of introducing myself causes those around me to respond in a very different way. Mercy of all mercies, I am never asked a tax question! Most people do not even ask me about busy season.

Instead, the conversation generally moves in the direction of family, community activities or business. Amazingly enough, I usually demonstrate at least a limited ability to discuss something other than accounting or tax. Also since my name is a part of the firm name, I believe a subliminal communication occurs to the effect that our accounting firm may be more than just an accounting firm. If you help perpetuate the stereotype of a bean counter, chances are good that is what most people will expect of you.

How do you get out of the box?

In January 1995, I illustrated the box syndrome by spending the first ten minutes of our second annual stakeholders' meeting in front of our people with a box over my head. Few people may have realized how truly difficult it is to make a presentation when so encumbered.

Let me explain. My voice was muffled, so no one could clearly hear what I was saying. Eye contact with my audience was severely limited, so no one could see me and I could see no one. My mobility was impaired, and my inability to maneuver with any agility provided an annoying distraction. Applied to our work, the lesson for our audience and for us, is that we keep ourselves boxed in, thereby hampering our progress and success.

To reinforce the need for our people to step out of the box, Karl Krumm began the afternoon session shuffling around the front of the room with both of his feet in the box. We both were uncomfortable for a few minutes, but we made our point!

*CPAs must begin thinking of and positioning ourselves to be the **preferred business advisor** to our clients.*

We must begin emulating the good family practitioner. We must develop a relationship with our clients that encourages them to call us when they have a headache. If we determine their headache requires brain surgery, then we will refer them to a good brain surgeon. Do not try brain surgery, even if the book is in the library. We may need to be present as the assisting physician for the diagnosis and surgery. If our assistance is not required, we should visit our patient during their recovery and assist in their rehabilitation.

In addition to becoming the preferred business advisor to our clients, we need to assume the role of broker for business or financial services. For too many years, we have responded to phone calls from clients and prospects with an apologetic explanation that we do not offer a particular service. We then let it drop. Sometimes, we referred our client to another professional without ever following up to see how the project went.

To become an effective broker of services requires forming strategic alliances with other professionals--personal financial planners, investment managers, attorneys, bankers, bookkeeping services, computer technicians and other service providers.

Some of our traditional competitors will become allies. Learning to successfully form these alliances allows us to effectively compete with the "big guys." Often it provides the "little guy" a competitive advantage.

Strategic alliances and core values--Trust.

By now you may be getting sick of the word trust, but there are many reasons to instill trust into your organization. The nature of strategic alliances requires sharing in a project so all parties benefit.

Sharing requires trust. Without this, the alliance will not succeed. Many organizations are not willing to share trust to the extent necessary to effectively form an alliance. This may be why many accounting firms are not participating in significant strategic alliances. Trust is critical when entering an alliance with one or more of your competitors. We have excelled in this area.

When someone asks how our firm differentiates itself, I respond that no other firm in town can say their biggest referral source for new business is other CPA firms.

This powerful statement is true because several of the largest CPA firms in town trust our work and trust we will not steal theirs. I have never understood why people would bite the hand that feeds them, but many do.

Two of the Big Six firms refer work to us that does not fit their economic model.

In most cases they have been serving these clients, but have decided the client relationship is not providing sufficient profit margins and a public offering is not on the immediate horizon. The work is transferred to us with the understanding that should a public offering occur, we will return the client to them. Our audit work is trusted to the extent the Big Six firm does not expect to replicate any of our work, should they reenter the scene. These client referrals, which generally result in annual fees of $10,000 to $15,000, are the bread and butter of our practice. We do a great job of serving this client profile.

Several local firms refer significant work to us.

Three of these are tax firms, employing six to eighteen people, that do not perform audit services or some of the business consulting services we perform. In five or six client situations we have a continuing alliance where we perform audit and/or consulting services. The referring firm continues to perform tax services for our common client. For four other full service firms, we have alliances where we perform second partner reviews of audit reports, share professional staff when necessary and provide advice on technical issues. In some situations we have been doing this for four or five years and it has worked remarkably well.

We have not had one experience of any firm in an alliance getting greedy or stealing a client.

As a result of the nine strategic alliances with CPA firms, in 1996 we performed $140,000 in recurring services and over $150,000 in consulting services. Not bad, considering that five years ago we had no dialogue at all with these competitors.

A positive aspect of these client relationships is they have all been obtained without a competitive proposal process. In turn, we refer to these firms services we have decided not to offer. Another by-product has been the relatively free exchange of information related to managing our respective accounting practices. Also, these alliances provide potential for future acquisitions or mergers.

International Strategic Alliances: AFAi

We joined Accounting Firms Associated, inc. (AFAi), an alliance of fifty-six independent accounting and consulting firms in the United States and an international affiliate with offices in ninety countries. The alliance provides ML&R a network of worldwide expertise and contacts, geographic dispersion, excellent technical resources, various marketing resources, quality continuing professional education and the purchasing power of an international firm. The technical resources of AFAi allow us to consider penetrating industries or functional specializations that we would not attempt on our own. The overall benefit of AFAi is access to the resources of an international firm without sharing ownership or its related compensation and profit considerations. Sharing resources among AFAi firms is more dynamic and free flowing than in some, if not all, of the Big Six firms.

We have also formed strategic alliances with computer network specialists, law firms, stock brokers, asset managers, investment advisors, bankers, insurance agents, executive search firms and niche consulting firms. These alliances have traditionally been informal in nature and somewhat sporadic. However, we have a project underway to begin a database of key contacts, skill sets and capabilities of each of these partners.

We hope to bring more consistency to our referral process, which in the past has too often relied on the first service provider or two that came to mind. Databases of this nature provide better information from which to suggest appropriate matches. In the future, some of these strategic alliances will be formalized and joint venture efforts will occur more frequently. By the turn of the century, some of these strategic alliances will reside under a shared roof.

Strategic alliances and core values-- Open communication and flexibility.

These are qualities necessary for successful strategic alliances. ***Open communication*** between competitors is at first difficult, but without it the client suffers. ***Flexibility*** is important because each alliance is unique in nature. Each project is approached differently and results vary. The open communication necessary for success becomes easier over time, but the real test of the alliance occurs when the project becomes unprofitable. Unless the parties effectively communicate and offer flexibility (give and take), suspicion will prevail and the alliance will fail.

Chapter 9. Our Obligation to the Community--Giving and Receiving Much More

♦ At least four of our firm's seven core values are included in this statement ♦ One factor that distinguishes our involvement in the community is our character ♦ In community service work, don't do your job ♦ The search for spirituality in the workplace will bond community-builders of the future ♦ Building community means helping each other in the workplace, too ♦ I am not suggesting a focus on religion in the workplace, but people are spiritual beings with needs that have been ignored by employers ♦ The expert suggested inventorying community assets, rather than needs ♦ We are developing unique biographies of each individual in the firm ♦ How we volunteer ♦ What drives us

---

One of our firm's core values states that we are built on a foundation of people dedicated to actively participating in the *community.*

We are fortunate to have attracted a group of people who share this value. Anyone who is too self-centered to subscribe to this philosophy will be driven crazy by the culture. One of the first things you see upon entering our office is the community wall. This is a space about twenty feet long that is covered with certificates and plaques that have been presented to our firm by various community organizations.

One of the signs on the wall states:

> **"Commitment is what transforms a promise into reality. It is the words that speak boldly of your intentions. And the actions which speak louder than words. It is making the time when there is none. Coming through time after time, year after year after year. Commitment is the stuff character is made of; the power to change the face of things. It is the daily triumph of integrity over skepticism."**
>
> ***--Author Unknown***

At least four of our firm's seven core values are included in this statement.

It embodies much of what the people in our firm represent.

In our reception area, we proudly display our recognition as an inductee into the Austin Adopt-A-School's *Hall of Fame.* Only fifteen of the 2,000 business partners in this beneficial program have received this recognition.

The credenza in our conference room has many other recognitions of our firm's commitment to the community. We display these not to be boastful, but to encourage others to get involved. No one can pass our Director of First Impressions (receptionist) or get a cup of coffee in our kitchen without seeing evidence of a coming community event that a number of our people are supporting--bowl-a-thons, 24 hour relays, fun runs, telethons, popcorn and candy sales, etc. This kind of involvement is systemic and occurs without pressure from anyone, anyplace, in our structure. We are blessed by this environment. Individually and collectively, our people are making a huge difference in the community. By extension, we all benefit.

One factor that distinguishes our involvement in the community is our character.

We do not have a coordinated plan to penetrate influential boards. We do not join efforts to meet influential people ultimately to sell them our services. Instead, we join efforts we *believe* in and for which we have a *passion.*

We owe this kind of involvement to our community, which has many needs and has been good to us. We also recognize that there is no better training ground and forum for lifelong learning than that offered by the nonprofit community. Peter Drucker, Scott Peck, Stephen Covey, and of course, Peter Block, in his latest book, ***"Stewardship**: Choosing Service Over Self Interest"*--all emphasize the tremendous value of ***building community***.

In community service work, don't do your job.

When I was a staff accountant, someone advised me to adopt a rule of avoiding the unlimited number of community service positions of financial secretary, treasurer or auditor. He told me, "Unless you make a concerted attempt to avoid these positions you can assume as a CPA this is what you will always be expected to do." What a wise man he was. Over the years, I have adopted the philosophy of not accepting a board position, unless the organization understands I will not accept any of the roles typically assigned to CPAs.

Goodness knows ten to twelve hours of accounting related activities a day is enough without volunteering for more. I have learned much by seeking board roles unrelated to accounting. These roles have included strategic planning, marketing, fund-raising, serving as master of ceremonies for events, appearing in television commercials, learning how to handle myself in televised board meetings, lobbying local politicians for support, mentoring at-risk students, gardening with physically-challenged preschoolers, facilitating board retreats, presiding over boards and mediating frequent non-profit feuds.

Actually, I have received so much from what appears to be giving to the community that I have difficulty differentiating the giving from the receiving. Truthfully, I can no longer answer the question of how many hours a week I work. I sleep eight hours each night. Apart from this I can no longer separate making a living from community, church or family activities.

Service has become a life style.

Some may think this is a curse. I think it is a blessing and am thankful for these opportunities and life in general. I have been driven for most of my life by what I am becoming instead of by what I am doing. I believe this is why I never worried too much about some of the dreadful assignments I received as a young auditor. I tried to learn something from every experience.

Success for me has always been making the most of what you have, or the situation in which you find yourself. For the past several years, I have been driven by a spiritual search for purpose in my life. Community service, family and a relationship with God have provided more guidance than anything I have ever done to produce revenue for our firm. Granted, the revenue production has enabled many of the activities.

The search for spirituality in the workplace will bond community-builders of the future.

I believe in the next ten years, the search for spirituality in the workplace will become more widely accepted. Fewer people will be looking for a job and more people will be looking for work. Less will be looking just to get by, and more people will be looking for purpose in their lives. Fewer people will be looking for a place to do a job and more people will be looking for a workplace that provides a sense of community. For the first time in my life I feel our workplace is becoming a community that supports our people in their lives outside work. I believe it is beginning to meet the new definition of ***community***--*a place where three or more people periodically gather who share common values.* We may not be able to save the world. We may not even be able to solve the sometimes overwhelming problems in our metropolitan area. However, we can do something about our smaller spheres of influence--the workplace and our own families are certainly two of these.

Building community means helping each other in the workplace, too.

Our people help each other through times of financial need, death, illness, the trials and tribulations of parenting, and many other life challenges. Our people babysit for each others' children, help each other move furniture, lend money and vehicles to one another, sell cars and homes to one another, etc. You may believe this is true of most workplaces, but I sense our situation is something special. The sense of building community in the workplace is more critical than ever before.

Why is this?

The answer is simple. Many people have no other significant mechanism of support. Much of the traditional support structure providing a sense of community has disintegrated--families, neighborhoods, churches, etc. We must do something to support ourselves through the difficult journey.

If business leaders are really serious about redefining government--especially in the areas of welfare reform and health and human services--businesses should assume more responsibility for supporting their own people and those who surround them. It is obvious that government cannot effectively address these needs; and the past forty years of failed social policies prove it.

I am not suggesting a focus on religion in the workplace, but people are spiritual beings with needs that have been ignored by employers.

One of the things that will fuel this search for spirituality is the aging of 80 million Baby Boomers. The Boomers represent the largest group of unchurched people in history and many have been driven by a greed for material things.

As the Boomers age, they will begin to question the purpose of hustling simply to accumulate wealth. What has been the meaning of their lives? How did their lives become so misdirected? What have they contributed to the betterment of society?

I believe a sense of community is at the center of being able to respond positively to these questions. The attainment of a certain degree of spirituality in one's life will allow us to begin to discuss these things in the workplace and these discussions will become valued workplace benefits.

Tradition-minded human resource directors fear spiritual discussions in the workplace as much as they feared the idea of a family friendly workplace a decade ago.

I hope we overcome the fear.

Recently, I attended a presentation by a health and human services expert. He began his presentation by holding a glass of water that was partially full. Most people assumed he would ask how many people believed the glass was half full versus half empty. Instead, he simply said that for too long, our focus in health and human services was concentrated on the part of the glass that was empty. As a result, he noted, study after study and program after program focused on needs assessments, funding gaps, and what people did not have. Also, he suggested that such a focus on needs usually led communities and, more specifically, social workers, to being overwhelmed by the problems, which led to exhaustion, depression and burnout.

Historically, our public efforts in the health and human service areas have focused on the needs of the less fortunate. Programs were developed and implemented from the top and forced on communities and people that really needed help. Many programs completely missed the mark because the health and human resources programs were developed without completely understanding the consumers' culture.

The expert suggested taking an inventory of community assets, rather than needs.

The expert suggested a new approach, or attitude, that focused on whatever amount of water was in the glass. The ultimate goal of the new approach is the same as the old approach, to fill the glass. He encouraged our community leaders to begin shifting our focus from concentrating on needs to first taking an inventory of our community's assets and then determining how to best leverage them. This evolving attitude is more of a "bottom up" approach, than the traditional one. The old approach developed programs at "the top" and then communities decided if they wanted to apply for the program.

The expert told us how some communities had begun to go door to door in some of the nation's worst ghettos. The adult who answered the door was asked a few questions. These included, "What are the three things you do best and what kind of meetings do you attend?" The first question is a means of determining the talents of the people in the neighborhood. The second question identifies the organizations and associations that are active in the neighborhood. This question is important in locating vehicles that can be used to leverage individuals' talents.

An interesting thing has resulted from this approach. Many neighborhoods that appear to be wastelands are actually full of talented people who want to help restore a sense of community in their neighborhood. These people regularly meet with others. Many have formed organizations and associations which have not been apparent to outsiders or social workers, at least not until someone asked. Assets of the neighborhood are inventoried and the residents decide how to best leverage their own resources. The government effort is to assist and support the process, while providing resources to leverage the *already existing assets* of the neighborhood.

This model will not be the cure-all for our social ailments, but I am encouraged by the new attitude. It seems to be gaining support in the health and human services sector. I am intrigued by this proactive and common-sense approach to a huge set of problems.

I was so impressed by the clarity and purpose of community-building, I introduced some of the concepts to our firm.

The day after the expert's presentation, I altered my approach to an officewide meeting that had been scheduled for several weeks. I began the meeting by holding a partially full glass of water. Everyone expected the old line. Instead, I explained that for too long our organization had focused on the part of the glass that was empty. We consumed ourselves with fixing problems and focusing on our own shortcomings. I explained we were going to begin focusing on the part of our glass that was full.

Our goal would be to leverage our assets to maximize our potential, not to become exhausted by focusing on our shortcomings.

Our first step was to inventory the assets of our own people, the things they like best, and the things they most want to do with their careers. You may take for granted that a CPA firm would have a database of our people's assets and their resources. The truth is, we have never done a credible job of mapping our assets.

We are developing unique biographies of each individual in the firm.

As you would expect, the biographies include technical qualifications, industry expertise, college degrees and professional activities. What makes the biographies different is they focus on who our people are and what they are becoming--family activities, hobbies, interests, community involvement. A personal photograph is included which best depicts the person. These will be selected from personal family picture albums. I believe the exercise of finding just the right picture will produce some interesting results.

More important than mapping our assets, will be the change in our firm's *attitude*. We will concentrate on maximizing our assets instead of being overwhelmed by our problems. This may be the only idea we have borrowed from the public sector. I hope it works as well in our community at large as I believe it will for our community within the workplace.

How we volunteer.

Our people serve on over twenty-five community boards and countless church and family centered activities. This level of commitment has actually eased the difficulty in responding to the endless number of funding requests we receive. We explain to others that our people are so active in the community we are required to limit our financial support to those organizations. This is not just a good corporate line. It is the *truth*. When asked to do pro bono audit or tax work for a community organization, we decline. Then we suggest we might have someone in our office who would volunteer in their organization. These philosophies keep the door open for all of our people to become involved in their community.

We do not have a policy concerning community work--no guidelines for time off, or a list of approved organizations. Instead, people understand our firm's commitment to the community and determine the degree to which they become involved. In this way, the individual balances volunteer time with other demands, with support from the firm.

What drives us.

We are a ***relationships-driven*** firm. It seems every firm says that, but we are a firm that lives it.

As a result, we spend nothing on advertising. We do not have a firm brochure. We spend less than most firms on client or prospect entertainment. We have a large governmental practice, but our shareholders do not make political contributions for the purpose of maintaining or increasing our practice.

Simply, we are known for our community involvement and for our people who are not afraid to make commitments and then live up to them.

Our revenues have more than *doubled* within the past five years, during a period that has seen almost all the largest accounting firms in town shrink in size.

I attribute much of this to our presence in and commitment to the community.

Chapter 10. Attracting and Retaining the Best People in a Family Friendly Workplace

♦ How can your business support parents ♦ The family friendly workplace has become a frequent topic ♦ Our new firm decided to bring children to work if needed, and participate in their education ♦ Flexible schedules have empowered our families ♦ Before taking the plunge into flexible work schedules, be aware of the pitfalls ♦ The learning curve took two to three years ♦ Finding a workable scheme for both part-time and full-time workers was a challenge ♦ The ESP Board ♦ Our firm's social events have become more family oriented ♦ "NO SUCCESS AT WORK IS WORTH FAILURE AT HOME"

Earlier, I mentioned that we allowed parents to bring their children to work on days that created daycare issues such as Columbus Day, Presidents' Day and in-service training days for teachers--despite fears of disrupting the work environment and complaints from clients.

This was the beginning of creating a family friendly workplace.

During 1990 and 1991, when I chaired the local Adopt-A-School program, I became interested in the concept; however, at the time, the term ***family friendly workplace*** was not being used. Nonetheless, a group of people became interested in moving the business-education partnership of Adopt-A-School to a different level. The idea was to encourage businesses to support their employee parents in becoming more involved in their children's education. We believed employer support for programs that better equipped parents to participate in the educational experiences of their children offered both immediate and long-term benefits. This support not only enabled parents to be better workers, but also contributed to the well-being of tomorrow's adults and enhanced the nation's future labor force.

During our presentations to CEOs, we cited various factors that should influence their decision to participate:

A. In 1990, the PTA/Dodge National Survey asked: Why aren't parents more involved in schools?

72%	....	Not enough time
66%	....	Work conflicts
24%	....	Need child care
13%	....	Spouse already involved
5%	....	School discourages

B. Occupations of the future will require more education, which is illustrated as follows:

Current jobs:

6%	....	8 years or less
12%	....	1-3 years of high school
40%	....	4 years of high school
20%	....	1-3 years of college
22%	....	4 years of college or more

New jobs:

3%	....	8 years or less
10%	....	1-3 years of high school
35%	....	4 years of high school
22%	....	1-3 years of college
30%	....	4 years of college or more

C. Workers with dependent children at home:

42%	....	Children under 18
32%	....	Children under 13
18%	....	Children under 6

Workers with children under 13 at home:

65%	....	Employed spouses/partners
22%	....	Nonemployed spouses/partners
13%	....	Single-parent workers

Workers with any dependent care responsibilities
(child under 18, disabled adult, or elder) 47%

Workers with adult dependent or elder care responsibilities .. 8%

How Can Your Business Support Parents?

A. Let your employees know you believe their children's education, health, safety and self esteem are important.

B. Survey your employees about their parenting needs.

C. Encourage formation of peer discussion groups at the workplace for parent employees.

D. Share parenting information. Offer lunchtime seminars on childcare and parental topics.

E. Consider granting parental leave for meetings with children's teachers.

F. Assist employees in locating safe, stimulating and affordable child care.

G. Sponsor workplace literacy programs.

H. Consider offering flexible scheduling or job sharing.

I. Provide assistance to employees who need counseling or drug and alcohol treatment for their children.

J. Develop policies and programs which encourage parent involvement in children's well-being.

The first brochure of Austin's Adopt-A-School's **Employers Support Parenting** (ESP) program included these suggestions. We incorporated many of these in our early efforts to become more family friendly.

The family friendly workplace has become a frequent topic for business journals and periodicals.

This now seems like a fairly reasonable concept and has become widely accepted. However, in 1991, the topic was not very popular.

Some of the CEOs we approached, as Adopt-A-School volunteers, acted as if we were from the dark side of the moon. Several chose not to commit to joining the program and refused to sign the commitment form. They expressed concerns about litigation, union contracts, setting workforce precedents and all kinds of horror stories that could result from committing to support their employees as parents. Initially, the concept met a lack of acceptance and it was not until 1991-92 that we finally got ten or twelve companies and public sector organizations to agree to become part of the ESP pilot project.

As co-chair of this effort, I felt obligated to do something to demonstrate my commitment.

Our new firm decided to bring children to work if needed, and participate in their education.

We invited our people to bring their children to work when it made sense. This alleviated childcare issues and provided children with the chance to see Mom or Dad at work. When the children tired of shadowing their parent or playing on the computers, we microwaved popcorn, plugged in a video and the conference room became a mini-cinema.

In our administrative manual, we included the policy, "We expect our employees to participate in the education of their children. Reasonable paid time off will be provided to attend school events such as parent-teacher conferences, performances, athletic events, etc." Concerns about the inequity of offering this benefit when not

everyone had children were alleviated by expanding the definition of parenting. People were provided time to deal with issues surrounding aging parents, grandparents and/or grandchildren.

People without children were encouraged to become mentors in the Adopt-A-School program.

Since these early days we have moved much closer to a family friendly workplace. We offer a variety of flexible schedules. Twenty-eight percent of our people take advantage of this flexibility--six working mothers, a semiretired mother whose own mother is in her eighties, a man of sixty years who has begun seminary, and two college interns who work around their school schedules. No two flexible schedules are alike and I could not begin to repeat them. However, the mothers generally work from 8:30 a.m. to 2:30 p.m., eight or nine months of the year. They do not work during the Christmas holidays or summer months. Our *Director of First Impressions* spends the entire summer working on a ranch in Wyoming with her daughter. For staff members who are students, we insist school be scheduled first. Then we schedule work.

Why did we not think of and become serious about these flexible schedules before 1992?

We were stuck in our ways and believed a person was only valuable if we had unlimited access to and *control* over them.

Any time commitment of less than full-time indicated an employee's lack of loyalty or misguided priorities. Experience proves the flexible situation is a clear winner. The working mother remains active and technically current, has an income and is home for her school age children. The firm retains a talented person who is productive during our period of greatest need.

Before taking the plunge into flexible work schedules, be aware of the pitfalls.

Be aware of the learning curve and the time required to manage this foray into providing flexibility to a limited number of your associates. Initially, most of the resistance came from managers who always had access to everyone all the time.

What if a client called after the associate left work at the unusual time of 2:30 p.m.? What if they needed some information? What if no one responded when someone beckoned? How could we ever plan a meeting with all these crazy schedules?

The next resistance came from full-time colleagues. Some of these people resented the special deals offered to certain people. They also believed the cost of flexibility rested on the shoulders of the associates who worked the traditional full-time career track. Subconsciously, they found it difficult to wish someone a good evening when they knew the person who was leaving early had the benefit of an evening five or six hours longer than their own.

Finally, the part-timers felt guilty for leaving early. Early in their careers, they had worked the long hours of the traditional CPA career path. Under their new arrangement, they left unfinished work behind each day. At one time they would have felt obligated to stay until it was completed. Their departures often resembled someone sneaking away.

The learning curve took two to three years.

We first communicated to everyone our commitment to provide flexible part-time career tracks. The firm committed to doing its part to make these special deals work. If the firm's workload required more time than agreed to in a given part-time arrangement, we would hire additional staff to do the work. Most firms make the mistake of constantly looking to their part-timers to fill the gaps. Part-time arrangements usually fail because the part-time job becomes full-time, which is not what the worker wanted.

We also subscribed to our part-time associates being afforded the same status as full-time colleagues. This commitment extended to working space, business cards, continuing education, employee benefits, social events, participation on process teams, firm meetings, etc.

Finally, we constantly remind our people of the seasonality and the underlying economics of our practice, both of which dictate our strategy to offer part-time positions.

We offered the part-time arrangement to anyone in the firm who desired it. This reduced the resentment from detractors of the new program. Obviously, however, not everyone could afford the luxury of a part-time salary. Although change is difficult, our demonstrated commitment over two to three years proved most effective.

"***Chrono therapia***," or time therapy, when properly applied, usually works wonders, and in this case it was the best treatment.

Finding a workable scheme for both part-time and full-time workers was a challenge.

By 1995, very little or no time was spent discussing the merits of a part-time workforce. By the fall, I decided it was time to mix things up again. For some time, I recognized the need for something between the traditional and part-time career paths. More and more of our workforce were second income earners. Many of these situations involved a spouse who made considerably more than the accountant in the family. Many of these spouses worked for large companies that offered a regular forty hour week, weekends off and predictable vacations.

The traditional public accounting career path offered none of these features. Three months of the year required long hours, missed family dinners and weekend work. The other nine months provided hours that were unpredictable, with plenty of opportunities for getting home after dinner or working on Saturdays. Vacations were difficult to schedule, more difficult to take, and required constant telephone availability.

As I examined this issue, it occurred to me that six of the last eight people to leave our firm did so in order to take a forty hour-a-week job. Although people list several reasons for dissatisfaction in public accounting, the major one involved long and unpredictable hours. It occurred to me we had addressed this issue for the benefit of working mothers who could afford to work part-time. However, we had ignored the many people who wanted a challenging full-time job--one that provided the benefits of weekends off, dinners at home and predictable vacations.

I decided it made enormous sense to develop a system that provided people with a challenging and satisfying forty hour-a-week job. By now I had grown accustomed to relying on team dynamics for virtually all decisions. However, on this issue I decided to go it alone. I believed so strongly in this issue that I decided not to gain consensus from anyone.

In December 1995, I announced a new career track.

My plan was coupled with a new way of obtaining individual time commitments. Instead of "management" dictating acceptable billable and total hour commitments for each individual, each person was asked to develop their own time commitments. Each person was furnished a summary of the hours they charged in the previous year. They were furnished with average billable hours for each professional level and the range of total hours worked by full-time people (2,080 - 2,600).

Full-time people were asked to estimate their allocations of time by function for the coming year. Their total hour commitments were expected to be either 2,080 (forty hours per week), 2,330 (average 1995 total time) or 2,580 (the upper end of the 1995 range).

Over a two year period, base salaries would be adjusted to reflect the level of total commitment. However, during this period no one

This workplace supports families with flexible work schedules.

would take a pay cut for having the courage to reduce commitment. People were surprised at the apparent lack of direction because they were accustomed to being told how much they were expected to work. I told everyone to do their best.

When I received all the commitment forms, we compiled and communicated the results to the office.

The results were interesting:

- Total billable hours were within 1% of the total that would have been forced upon people under the traditional system.
- Career tracks were selected as follows:

Part-time ------- 8
2,080 hours ------- 1
2,330 hours ------- 12
2,580 hours ------- 12

Although initially only one person had the courage to select the forty hour a week track, in late 1996 two more people opted for this track. I predict that within three years, one-fourth of our people will have chosen the alternative track. Time will tell. In the meantime, we are committed to supporting our people as parents.

The ESP Board

We have an Employers Support Parenting ("ESP") brag board.

The ESP board is simply a $15 bulletin board in a common area where children's school accomplishments are prominently displayed. Items on the brag board are those treasures that are often found attached to home refrigerators.

This simple but effective tool does two things. First, it tells a child that school work is important enough for Mom or Dad to take it to work and show it off. Second, it allows us to learn more about each other and our families.

When the board overflows, someone removes an item or two that has been on the board for a while and returns it to the appropriate parent. No particular system or special rules have been necessary. Potential abuses were an early concern that never materialized.

Popularity of the concept caused us to buy a second board, thereby doubling available space. The boards are always full. Also, we display a collection of current periodicals and resource materials related to parenting issues. Discount coupons to amusement parks, family events and museums are available.

The ESP Board became more than a collection of what our *children* were doing--it is a symbol of what *we* as a *firm* are doing.

Our firm's social events have become more family oriented.

The traditional golf day outing and country club Christmas party were replaced by a family picnic and a Christmas party hosted in someone's home. The annual picnic, which is purposely old-fashioned, is held at the lake and features boating, fishing, skiing, swimming, egg tosses, three legged races, peanut scrambles, horse-shoes, volleyball and Texas barbecue. We hold Easter egg hunts and the office is always open to families for viewing holiday fireworks from one of the best locations in town--the 17th floor of an air conditioned, mosquito-free environment.

For many years, I hosted breakfast meetings. A morning person, I like to get up early and thought these meetings were most effective. In 1992, someone explained to me that breakfast meetings were not parent-sensitive. I was asked if I had ever had to make lunches, dress children, and deliver them either to school, the bus stop or the neighbor's house one hour earlier than normal. Since then I have not scheduled another breakfast meeting. We host brown-bag lunches where parenting issues are discussed. There is almost an unlimited number of organizations who furnish speakers on a variety of parenting issues, free of charge.

We encourage our people to take *family vacations.* I have never been impressed by anyone who tells me they have not had time to take a vacation in several years. Instead, I question their priorities or organizational abilities. How can business people, who pride themselves in managing million dollar projects, not find the time to manage a family vacation? One of my partners says he has never seen a luggage rack on a hearse. I have not seen one either. I cannot force a family vacation on everyone. However, I do set the tone by planning my next summer's vacation during every busy season.

Then, during the vacation, I leave my laptop computer at the office, resist listening to voice mail and do not call into the office. The office runs itself. People protect my time away. Upon my return, I do the same for them. I do not remember interrupting anyone's vacation because of an urgent office or client related matter. Protecting each others' time away pays big dividends for our people and for the firm as a whole.

The confidence of my actions is the greatest compliment I could pay the people in our organization. Also, successful implementation of the concepts described in this book contributes greatly to my confidence in leaving the office.

I remember the day I returned from a two week vacation. At my first meeting of the day, a business leader asked how I could be gone for two weeks if our firm was so busy. Briefly, I explained my philosophy.

"You sound proud of that," he said.

"I am," I replied.

He shook his head.

Soon our people will be working from home, or other remote locales. Remote processing technology has tremendous potential for addressing the latch key issue that is a concern to many of our people. Remote access will allow our people to work from home on certain days and reduce the stress caused by family illnesses, deaths, plumber visits, etc.

What are the benefits of supporting a family friendly workplace to our firm?

- Absenteeism decreased.
- Morale increased.
- Productivity improved.

We also found productivity during shadowing experiences was 80 percent better than when Mom or Dad stayed at home and called in sick. Flexible work arrangements allow us to retain talented people once forced out of public accounting. Turnover has been significantly reduced.

In five and a half years, no full-time person has left our firm to join another CPA firm.

We hope to contribute positively to our families' mental health and to our children's chances of better achieving their potential. Our workplace has become more productive. Recruiting talented people to our firm has become easier. Most of all, offering a flexible work environment is the right thing to do for out firm and our families!

I admire family advocate Ona Porter who says:

"NO SUCCESS AT WORK IS WORTH FAILURE AT HOME."

This is something I challenge companies and organizations to embrace when I speak to them about the importance of supporting our families through the workplace. This has become one of my personal missions.

Dear Daddy,
I haven't seen you a lot
lately. How are you
doing? I am getting so
big.
would
No Success
at Work
is worth
Failure
at Home

Chapter 11. Motivating Your Partners in Profits

- ◆ A ten year history of our attempts to find the perfect supplemental compensation
- ◆ The benefits of profit sharing have impacted the mind set of everybody in the firm

---

Before beginning the section on motivating your partners in profits, it is important to review the recent history of supplemental compensation systems. For purposes of this discussion, we must set the stage for the events leading to profit sharing before we jump into the mechanics of our profit sharing plan.

The formula itself takes only two minutes to explain.

Of all the reengineering efforts described in this book, the step toward profit sharing is one of the last to take. To begin profit sharing ***before*** implementing teamwork, instilling trust through open book management, involving everyone in the budgeting process and laying the groundwork for self-directed careers is a recipe for ***disaster***.

A ten year history of our attempts to find the perfect supplemental compensation:

1986 - 1991

The Big Six firm used a ***performance-driven*** system based on achievement of individual goals. The distribution was determined by the partner in charge of the office. Only partners and managers participated in the bonus plan.

The strength of this system was that it forced people to prepare individual goals and provided a target for achievement.

Weaknesses included sandbagging by participants, slowing down upon achievement of significant goals--creating a false ceiling of accomplishment--and achieving individual goals at the expense, or to the detriment, of the firm as a whole.

Finally, the allocation of the bonus pool was fairly arbitrary.

1991 - 1992

ML&R used a performance-driven system based on ***formulas*** determining supplemental compensation for shareholders and senior associates. The distribution was also decided by formula, with some room for judgment by the shareholder group.

Strengths of the system included the establishment of individual goals with input from colleagues and the removal of subjectivity from the distribution.

Weaknesses revolved around formula-driven people who made decisions that improved their chances with the formula. Other people, who were more concerned with doing the right thing, ignored the formula and were penalized.

Finally, the formula assumed firm profits and the ability of the firm to pay bonuses, which did not actually occur until year three of the firm.

Associates used a performance-driven system of personnel evaluations to determine the individual allocation of a predetermined bonus pool. The bonus pool was guaranteed to be 7.5 percent of base salaries, with kickers if the firm achieved certain levels of net income. No individual was guaranteed any amount. However, at least 7.5 percent of total base salaries would be distributed to the associate group.

Strengths of the system included a decent feedback and counseling system and a performance incentive to achieve.

Weaknesses included the 7.5 percent guarantee. During the first two years of the firm's existence, we had to borrow money to fulfill that obligation. Management's morale declined as we received no bonus and had to borrow to pay associates. Only an accounting firm would have devised something like ***this!***

Another weakness was that the system created an environment of competition within the firm.

1993 - 1994

We used a performance-driven system based on achievement of individual goals. Shareholders and senior associates presented goals to the management group at the beginning of the year and reviewed progress at midyear. The entire management group voted year-end bonuses for each individual based on achievement of individual goals. The voting technique was called the "paper slip method."

Strengths of the system included immediate feedback from peers. Also, it was difficult to argue with the collective votes of seven or eight of your closest colleagues. The associates continued the system described for the 1991 - 1992 period.

1995 - Current

Recently, we implemented an officewide, ***profit sharing*** system. At the beginning of each year, the shareholders determine market-driven salaries for themselves and the senior associates. The senior associates determine the same for associates and support staff. Raises are driven by performance.

At the end of the year, one half of net income is distributed to the entire office. If the amount is 10 percent of firm's base salaries, then everyone gets 10 percent of their base salary as a profit sharing distribution. The remainder of net income is retained for debt service, capital additions and working capital.

When the Human Resources Team recommended an officewide profit sharing system in late 1994, I was surprised. I had considered this on several occasions, but lacked the nerve to suggest it. I did not believe an appropriate level of trust existed for people to rely on management's financial statements, reserves, etc. to determine their distributions.

The team's recommendation demonstrated more trust and camaraderie than I thought existed. I was both pleased and frightened that one of the teams had gotten ahead of my own calendar. Up to this point everything associated with the new firm had progressed at a slower pace than I desired. I did not know what to think of this. Also, for many years I had been a staunch proponent of performance-driven bonus systems.

A profit sharing system seemed to represent something between socialism and communism. I was not sure I wanted to invite that into our home. Since then I have changed my mind. I have grown to believe the story of America being built on rugged individualism is a myth that was sold to the public for several generations. Now, I believe America was built by small groups of people with shared values who periodically came together to build homes, roads, dams, etc.

In reality, little of consequence was built by lone rangers. The myth of rugged individualism, in a sad way, has contributed to the degeneration of our communities. At one time, communities were defined as groups of three or more people with shared values who gather to work toward common goals. As a society, I believe we need to restore this definition. The workplace and home is the place to begin.

The benefits of profit sharing have impacted the mind set of everybody in the firm.

The benefits of profit sharing have been significant, and nothing else has changed the mind set of the entire group as much as this concept. People are anxious to receive current financial statements to see how we did, and whether the expected distribution increased or decreased. The 1995 distribution was 6 percent of base salaries. *In 1996, we distributed 12.5 percent of base salaries.*

A dynamic exists in this respect that has not existed before.

Revenue generation and service efficiencies, combined with value, receive attention like never before.

The turf battles that dominate so many firms are virtually nonexistent in ours. We operate as a ***unit.*** Many firms our size operate as four independent practices working under the same roof--sharing space, overhead and people. Profit sharing contributes to selling and growing as a team. Since everyone benefits from profitable growth, this becomes a common goal of every individual. Little time is spent worrying about who gets credit for a success.

Also, our culture does not encourage anyone to restrict access to "their" clients. All clients are clients of the firm, and therefore have access to all its people and resources.

Expenses are watched like never before, and by every employee.

Contracts that have been taken for granted in the past--printing, plant services, delivery services, office supplies, computers and laser cartridges, to name a few, have been reexamined. Cost savings have been significant. Diskettes are now being reformatted. Last year our accountants threw away several hundred dollars' worth of diskettes, until the Common Area Team leader suggested a recycling box for diskettes. The budgeting process received unprecedented attention from each of the process teams and, as a result, cost savings continue. Everyone is in the act.

During the past four years, total revenues have doubled, fees per hour have increased by 40 percent and profits per shareholder have increased significantly.

Something tells me we may never be the same again.

Chapter 12: Where Are We on Our Journey? Where Are We Headed?

◆ Recent successes ◆ Pritchett on people committing to their jobs; ambiguity, uncertainty; willingness to embrace change ◆ Astounding results of treating people differently ◆ PROCESS TEAMS ◆ "Continual improvement" more than just a buzz word ◆ ECONOMICS OF THE FIRM ◆ On new proposals ◆ Immediate goals ◆ Mining the Internet ◆ Future virtual office ◆ Sounds easier than it will be ◆ The Redefinition Team, ***Lotus Notes***™ groupware and paperless audits ◆ Accountants changing their spots ◆ Marketing courses ◆ Problems don't mean failure ◆ We will find a way ◆ Our story, "warts and all" ◆ General Performance Expectations from the Human Resources Team ◆ Gender training ◆ Where are we headed?

Recently our firm celebrated its sixth anniversary. It has been three and one half years since we began our serious conversion effort. This clock began to run when we hired outside expertise to speed and direct our effort.

Clearly, the first benefits of the conversion were intangible, but during the past year we have begun to realize some observable benefits.

The journey toward reengineering the accounting firm model has been the most difficult thing I have done.

It has taken far longer than I expected and we still have far to go. When we began the journey in 1991, I expected the cultural conversion to take two years. If a test had been administered then, we may have received a grade of 30 percent. After six years we might score 80 percent. Finally, I understand the basic premise of continual improvement; that this process is something that is always occurring and never complete. Now my goal is to move the organization toward a consistent 90 to 95 percent score. Although we have become a passing student, we need to become an "A" student.

We are making progress.

First, I regularly receive compliments from clients and visitors about the friendly spirit of our office. They tell me it has a different feel than most professional service firms. I sense the same thing, although admittedly I am a bit biased. There is a camaraderie among our people that I have not previously seen in an accounting firm.

Second, barriers to teamwork and cooperation have diminished. Internal competition has almost disappeared. Our people are willing to help each other and, in turn, seem to take a different approach to helping clients. We have become a less selfish organization than in the past, while becoming more profitable (both tangibly and intangibly).

Third, because our people have become more active in the community, we attract a different kind of accountant--***real*** people who are not stereotypical accountants. Two or three years ago, our recruiting efforts focused on technical abilities. Now, our recruiting focuses more on determining the person's suitability to operating in our redefined and constantly changing culture. We have learned that unselfish people make good service providers. It is easier to teach technical skills than values, attitude, commitment and willingness to embrace change.

Fourth, treating people differently means we achieve nearly perfect attendance at firm events. People enjoy visiting with colleagues and their families on a social basis. Also, firm alumni attend our social events. This occurs so often that we find it unnecessary to hold special alumni events.

Our recruiting efforts are increasingly focused on attracting people who understand and embrace the realities we face as we enter the information age. This presents a challenge, because as a rule, accountants' dispositions and training do not prepare them to become what Price Pritchett describes in *The Employee Handbook of New World Habits for a Radically Changing World.*

For example, on the **importance of people committing fully to their jobs**, Pritchett wrote:

> Expect your employer to expect more from you. The reason? The marketplace is demanding far more these days from the organization itself. In times past, the most common solution to problems was just to hire more employees. Spend more money. But companies can't afford that approach any more. Instead of throwing more people at problems, organizations now throw fewer. They have to do more--faster and better--with less. This calls for highly committed people. There's no room for employees who mainly put in their time, going through the motions but giving only halfhearted effort. The people who seemed to keep their jobs merely because they could 'fog the mirror' are goners. In today's world career success belongs to the committed. To those who work from the heart...who invest themselves passionately in their jobs...and who recommit quickly when change reshapes their work.

Concerning **ambiguity and uncertainty,** Pritchett stated:

> ...so work roles will be a little out of focus much of the time. Careers won't be as clear cut as they used to be. And this is not happening by choice. The world is forcing our hand. A rapidly changing world deals ruthlessly with organizations that don't change, and people are coming to respect that fact. For your part, you need to respect the fact that a blur of ambiguity is actu-

ally in the best interest of your career. Perpetual change will be crucial if the organization is to survive in the years to come...Since you'll be going on guesswork to some extent, your ability to tolerate ambiguity and uncertainty will still stand as a 'critical skill.' So learn to loosen up. Prepare to feel your way along into the future. Be willing to 'wing it.' Develop your ability to improvise--even reduce it to an art form. And simply accept the fact that your work life is going to be fuzzy around the edges.

And on the **willingness to embrace change**, Pritchett wrote:

> You need to know that resistance to change is almost always a dead-end street. The career opportunities come when you align immediately with new organizational needs and realities. When you're light on your feet. When you show high capacity for adjustment. Organizations want people who adapt--fast--not those who resist or psychologically 'unplug.' Granted, change can be painful. When it damages careers, emotions such as grief, anger, and depression come naturally, making it hard for people to 'buy in' and be productive. But being a quick-change artist can build your reputation, while resisting change can ruin it. Mobility, not mourning, makes you a valuable member of the group. Shoot for rapid recovery. Instant alignment. Take personal responsibility for adapting to change, just like you would if you accepted a new job with a new employer.

The results of treating people differently are astounding.

On the alumni front, in over five years no full-time associate has left our firm to go to work for a competitor.

On the recruiting front, ten of our last thirteen recruiting offers have been accepted. Two people who declined our offers decided not to accept a position with any public accounting firm. We lost the third person to a Big Six firm, but with the option to return after she has received a couple of years of the world's best training. In 1996, she accepted a position with our firm after spending a year with the Big Six firm.

For the past two years, our annual turnover rate has averaged less than 10 percent, considerably less than the industry average. We have not experienced what we have previously seen on CPA bulletin boards, "Would the last person to resign, please turn off the lights?"

Since 1993, we generally have not counseled anyone to leave the firm. Instead, people have made career decisions on their own terms. In most cases, shareholders and associates recognized the person's decision to leave the firm months before the change actually occurred. This attrition happened in spite of our decision two years ago to abandon periodic performance reviews and counseling sessions. We still have quite a way to go in this area.

PROCESS TEAMS

The accomplishments of our Process Teams have exceeded my expectations! Chapter 6 chronicled these many accomplishments. In preparation for our 1996 third annual stakeholders' meeting, I prepared a chart of the major events of the firm's first five years.

Of the eighteen major events listed, half of these accomplishments occurred during 1995. The major events in 1996 *doubled* those of the previous year--a sure sign we are really beginning to realize successes. Why? The answer is very simple. The process teams are actively functioning. Continual improvement has clearly become more than just a buzzword.

Administrative improvements are occurring at a rate that is unheard of in a professional service firm. There is no shortage of innovative ideas. People are eager to participate. The challenge has moved from getting people to express ideas to being sure the list of projects does not exceed our ability to implement them. We have not needed a suggestion box in *over three years.*

Some organizations start every meeting with a $100 bill prominently clipped to the flip chart. The money goes to the person who suggests the first "bad" idea. This may be effective in many organizations. However, we do not have to bribe anyone in our office for innovation. The ideas flow naturally.

Also, we do not feel the need for special awards, sales commissions, or employees of the month. More importantly, the improvements are meeting the litmus test of, "Does the change improve either the work environment or service to clients?"

Finally, the improvements of the past five years have occurred while ***administrative costs*** as a percentage of revenues have ***decreased*** and ***billable hours per person*** have ***increased***. Also, billable hours per shareholder have increased. All of these positive things have happened, in spite of our people spending so much time in process team meetings. ***These are important benchmarks because the results of spending so much time in team meetings are the opposite of what most CPA partners expect--that billable hours would have decreased.*** What a wonderful situation to be in!

Economics of the Firm

We are well-positioned in our marketplace. Although we spend little on advertising and do not have a firm brochure, the business community probably knows us better than any other local CPA firm. I attribute this to our commitment to the *community*. Our people serve on over twenty-five civic boards. The activities of Adopt-A-School, Junior Achievement, Rotary Club, Easter Seals, Big Brothers & Sisters, Boy Scouts and many others touch the lives of all our people as well as our clients, who also participate in many of these community activities. These experiences offer more lifelong learning opportunities to our people than they can find anywhere, with the possible exception of marriage.

Most of our referrals come from CPA firms. This is a unique selling point because no other firm in town can make this statement. I attribute this to the trust factor the early TQM efforts instilled.

Our second largest referral source is existing clients. These referrals usually mean that we do not have to directly compete with other firms. Often these situations do not require us to prepare competitive proposals--a time consuming and costly process.

We closely examine requests for proposals and other opportunities before deciding to accept or reject them. Unless we have an established relationship with one of the decision makers in the selection process, we do not usually pursue the opportunity.

Another pre-qualifying procedure determines whether the opportunity clearly fits within the firm's strategic business plan, or its "Aim." This pre-analysis process saves on our investment in time and money. As a result, our *acceptance* rate on the proposals we submit to prospective clients has *increased* from 30 percent in 1993 to 70 percent in 1996.

In 1996, we declined more new client opportunities than we accepted. This philosophy has resulted in fewer bad debts, which have averaged less than .5 percent of annual revenues during the past four years.

- ***Our revenues have more than doubled during the past five years.***
- ***Fees per hour have increased by 40 percent, largely because of value-added services quadrupling.***
- ***Net income in 1996 was five times the amount recorded in our next best year--1995.***
- ***Our profits per shareholder increased 40 percent from 1995 to 1996.***

On the cost side, the effects of our officewide profit sharing have been significant. We scrutinize spending decisions like never before. Everyone participates. I am extremely proud of this spirit. I directly participate in only a few of these efforts--which makes it even more gratifying for me. Recently, someone asked if we had a purchase order system. We do. We call it *profit sharing.* Everyone now has a vested interest in achieving cost savings and receiving real value for every dollar spent.

TECHNOLOGY TEAM

Our current list of projects is lengthy and substantive. Here is what we are currently attempting:

In the summer of 1996, we made our first major investment in technology since 1994. That year we spent $80,000 to upgrade our computer resources. Since then, we have added several computers to our fleet and upgraded to Pentiums with better graphics using more color. Our recent focus has been on remote access and the Internet, which cost *over $60,000.* Although the dollar amount was not as large as what we invested in 1994, it was by far the most complex technology effort undertaken by our office.

The engine driving this change is ***Lotus Notes***™ and, although implementation of this product is not for the faint of heart, the opportunities created by *Notes*™ are immense.

Our immediate goals are to:

1. Install technology which enables our people to work from home, or anywhere else.

Although we do not anticipate all our people will do their work at home, our goal is for everyone to have the choice to work from home when it makes sense. Some people will make these choices to help address the issues of latchkey children, two hour commutes, etc. Others will make these choices for the same reasons this book is being written at home. This will be our first major step toward the virtual office, will lead us to redefine our operations, and will require us to release even more control over when and where people work.

Ultimately, this change may move us from billing by the hour to billing by the project. This may provide the answer to our clients who do not believe we have any idea how much time projects actually take. In reality, we never have.

Another potential impact of remote access is more of our associates will begin functioning as independent contractors charging by the project. On one hand, this is a frightening proposition. On the other, I believe most people will continue to view the resources and safety net of a large organization as beneficial.

People will continue to desire the socialization process offered by a group. We have thirty-eight people working in the space that was once occupied by twenty. Although there is a temptation to lease additional space, we have decided to continue with the space we have.

Our belief is that our work habits will change to such a degree that we will require considerably less space per person within the next year.

2. Take the first major step toward electronically linking ourselves to our clients and marketplace through the Internet.

E-mail has greatly enhanced our ability to communicate with clients and with each other. Electronic linking will eventually allow us to access our clients' financial and operational information from our office, or from *wherever* our workstations are! This feature will revolutionize the way tax returns are prepared and audits are conducted. The nature and importance of our physical presence will change. The process of preparing tax returns and conducting audits will move from an *historical* focus to an *on-line* focus. Eventually, accountants will become more useful in assisting companies in planning for the future.

Internet features receiving the most publicity include the world-wide web and related home pages. We have developed a handsome home page and will take advantage of the related marketing benefits as we better understand them.

The benefits of unlimited access to information and research are enormous and will benefit our firm and our clients. Access to information once reserved for the Big Six firms will be available to any one with electronic capabilities. *Eventually, our firm will become one of the leading information brokers in one of the largest industries of the future.*

Clients will pay us large sums of money to sift through huge amounts of information, analyze it and present them the best decision-making choices.

3. Maximize the use of technology which has been available for several years.

We are having difficulty getting our people to use technology--graphics, color overheads, computer-aided visuals, etc.--in their client presentations. This is baffling to me, since interest in and knowledge of technology exists. We are still using time constraints as an excuse and have not committed ourselves to making technology-aided presentations part of the normal audit or tax return process.

In addition, our people are generally not visual learners and do not appreciate that most of their clients are more comfortable with graphics than strings of numbers. This implementation failure is a weakness we must convert to a strength, and this conversion is beginning to occur.

Our Technology Team continues to work on these projects. As with our major technology upgrade in 1994, the Noname Team approved the estimated capital spending and broad philosophies of the projects. As we learned to do in 1994, our next step will be to practice staying out of the way of the Technology Team.

The Common Area Team coordinated the renovation of our office in 1995. Their next task is planning how our office should look in the near future. Time and money constraints dictate this project be implemented later. The physical layout of our office must support the efforts of teamwork and the virtual office of the near future. Our traditional layout of individual window offices and interior individual workstations provides privacy and status and contradicts everything this book is about.

Work has begun on the virtual office of our future.

In 1996, the Common Area Team began the planning for this change. No one knows how the new picture will look, but I suspect it will feature no walls, team seating in groups of three or four--instead of one--and numerous small conference rooms.

Other projects are longer term in nature.

Next year, we will buy the technology necessary to scan the documents in a file room full of paper. We can spend quite a bit of time and effort on this project before we use the more than $18,000 we annually spend to store files. Ultimately, we must invest in an integrated financial and operational system that is clearly aligned with the "Aim" of our firm.

For the past two or three years, we have tweaked our internal nonintegrated systems to more closely align them with our new approach. However, the results of our tweaking do not come close to meeting our needs, and the software cannot be purchased from the shelf. Not many firms are operating under our model so there is not much demand for a product that includes a scheduling system (data base) that supports the Atomic Model described in the next chapter.

Failure to have a scheduling system that supports a seamless approach to client service is a serious weakness--one we are addressing.

Client Service - Marketing Team

The Client Service-Marketing Team responded to a tall order in 1996. Rather than specific projects, this team attempted significant systemic change to our business culture. Of the seven major strategies listed as goals at our 1996 annual stakeholders meeting, four were the responsibility of this team:

- **Redefine service delivery--deliver seamless services.**
- **Focus on planning and eliminating rework.**
- **Radically increase consulting revenues.**
- **Proactively market our services.**

The first two items have been examined for the past year by a special task force known as the Redefinition Team. The research and brainstorming phase of the taskforce has been finished and the implementation phase will eventually be merged with the efforts of the ***Client Service-Marketing Team.***

The basic idea is to push the process team model that has been so successful in implementing internal change at ML&R into *client service projects.*

During the next year or two, we will implement this process team driven model in about 100 of our multi-service client locations. In the past, we called these audit clients.

The benefits of the new service delivery approach will give us a distinct advantage over our competition. Over a period of time, department barriers will fall. Clients will benefit from *seamless services.* Inexperienced associates will gain knowledge of the service delivery process once reserved for people with over five years of experience. Clients will have more than one or two people at ML&R who know enough about their operations to be valuable to them. Another benefit to the firm will be the elimination of rework, an enormous expense that, strangely, has been accepted for years as a cost of doing business. In the future, the same concepts will be applied to our 800 individual tax clients.

IBM recently announced a new computer chip that runs three times faster than today's speediest.

Many other changes are coming at us faster than we can accommodate them. To forecast future business issues, we must create better tools.

Yet, economists and business people continue to use graphs of the past five years to forecast future trends. This won't yield a true enough prediction anymore.

I believe that by changing our service delivery model we will become better-equipped to create our future.

This may sound easier than it will be.

The effort will be much more difficult than any alteration we have made because this fundamental change cuts to the core of what we do. Our people will probably respond in a way similar to that of the 1991 through 1993 period when we were beginning our reengineering efforts. Some will embrace the change and live to see the benefits of improved client service and increased profits to the firm. Others will be pushed to their very limits to make the required changes to their habits. A third group may be unwilling or unable to adapt to the significant changes and will leave the firm.

This is unfortunate, but it is reality.

The Redefinition Team has utilized Lotus Notes™ groupware to develop and pilot two paperless audits.

The national accounting firms are attempting to accomplish the same concept, which is to replace acres of audit workpaper files with data that is stored electronically. Many people see the benefits of this effort as reduced file management time and space, which is significant.

However, we are beginning to see much more now that we have had two initial experiences. From a project management standpoint, the ability to electronically access work in process on a daily basis presents a tremendous benefit. For the project managers, remote access to this knowledge enables them to remain current without physically being at the job site. More important, when they arrive on the job site they already have the knowledge to immediately interact with the client.

This sure beats the old days when managers appeared in the client's office and immediately buried themselves in a stack of audit workpapers in an attempt to learn enough about the project status to participate in a somewhat intelligent conversation with the client. We have just touched the tip of the iceberg in this new direction. The next hurdle will be *paperless tax returns.* Just imagine the powerful potential of this innovation!

Radically increasing consulting revenues directly impacts our future. It is significant because its successful implementation will result in ML&R becoming our clients' ***preferred business advisor.*** Currently, our clients think of us as the CPA who audits their books or prepares the tax returns. This effort will enable ML&R to become the ***preferred information broker*** in Central Texas, which will become a huge revenue source in the future.

Proactive marketing of firm services augments everything discussed to this point. This strategy was developed through a series of marketing sessions during a three to four month period. The sessions were structured for the personal benefit of every individual in our firm and for the ultimate benefit of the organization.

Courses offered were:

♦ **Networking in the Community**--This seminar addressed the four steps of networking: (a) making the most of events; (b) tools of the trade; (c) choosing a networking organization; and (d) courting prospective clients. Much of effective networking is just common sense, something we can easily overlook in today's hyperactive lifestyles.

♦ **Principles of Professional Service Marketing**--This session looked at similarities and differences between industrial marketing techniques and those applicable to professional service firms. Each participant was assigned a commercial services or industrial marketing article to present to the class. The presentations explored the thesis of the article, compared or contrasted the presenter's own opinion of its validity, and argued the applicability of the thesis to the ML&R business process.

♦ **Understanding the Call Process**--This session reviewed the techniques used in preparing for and implementing successful client, prospect or referral visits. Research before the call, the call process, and responsible follow-up actions were discussed.

Accountants changing their spots: How our marketing education comes to life.

We have completed the *Networking in the Community, Marketing Principles*, and *Understanding the Call Process* courses. The *Networking in the Community* course was taught by independent consultants who are network strategists.

The *Marketing Principles* classes were taught by our Director of Marketing and required each of four participants to be responsible for 25 percent of the class time and content. Articles were assigned in advance with instructions on meeting course expectations. Care was taken to ensure each student's article complemented, but did not duplicate, articles assigned to the other three participants.

A typical class included differentiation, zero defection, service recovery, and service guarantee related issues. During the course of these sessions, over 90 percent of our people participated on a voluntary basis. Our people came to the classes well-prepared and eager. Several worlds opened in front of them as issues were discussed. Our people began to see themselves as more than just accountants doing tax or audit work.

The typical accountant began to feel a part of the business process from which we are successfully growing our consulting practice. They are becoming more comfortable discussing marketing issues within the firm as well as with clients. This gives them self confidence in discussing a *holistic* approach to the business process.

All in all, the benefits to the marketing culture of the firm are significant.

The third course, *Understanding the Call Process*, took on a more pragmatic tone as it addressed the techniques of client calls. It, too, had an expectation for class participation including an exercise in which participants initiated a substantive business conversation. The assigned articles, and how those articles related to the client's business and/or industry, became the basis for the proposed conversations.

Throughout the classes we placed great emphasis on introductions. Introducing ourselves as individuals and as a firm in a way which distinguished us from other accounting firms became the genesis of our relationship building effort.

We will continue offering marketing courses during the next year.

The model of offering training sessions of four to six participants over a period of time has been successful. This should enable us to improve ourselves over a period of time. Substantial momentum seems to be sustained when similar topics are presented to a number of people over a period of time.

A traditional class offered to twenty to thirty-five participants sometimes results in significant momentum. However, the momentum is difficult to sustain because of ineffective follow up mechanisms. Six months later, people agree the course was interesting, but are disappointed it was not effective in creating change.

The concept of offering mini-courses to a number of people over a period of time has recently been extended to introducing the Atomic Model to our office. We plan to extend the model to present topics such as gender issues, improved communications and effective feedback.

Two other marketing related courses are being formulated and will be presented this year. *Implementing Appreciation Visits* will identify clients and prepare for specific visits. Included will be establishing the objective of each visit, discussing how to achieve honest appraisals of our work product, and learning to recognize new opportunities within the client's business and industry for both the client's and the firm's benefit. Each class will determine the calling personnel and will rehearse the planned call through role playing. *Preparing for a Presentation* will rehearse the introduction, theme, arguments, bridging, and closing of an effective group presentation. Each class member will prepare and make an actual presentation to the class.

Human Resouces Team

The Human Resources Team's focus has been to significantly *crank up* communications in the office. This effort included the following sub-topics:

- **Recognize someone daily.**
- **Activate the mentoring teams.**
- **Address gender-racial issues.**

The Human Resources Team has not made significant progress in either of the first two strategic items listed. In 1995, we scrapped our formal performance review and counseling system.

This system was the centerpiece of the traditional CPA culture. However, it never really worked--at least with respect to timely and honest feedback or sincere career counseling. It did produce evaluation and counseling forms that appeared in the personnel department every six months, just before the biannual salary review committee meetings. The system's major shortcomings were the lack of timeliness and sometimes dishonesty of the feedback.

However, the salary review committee process was a bright spot. It provided a forum where select management of the firm discussed the performance and potential of each staff member and made salary and promotion decisions.

In 1995, we replaced the formal performance and review system with one that assumed the following:

♦The *open book management* style of ML&R and a focus on open communication that encouraged an environment where constant feedback would become the norm.

♦*Mentoring teams* which would provide the forum for people to periodically meet with a group of people of various experience levels. At these meetings individual goals and aspirations would be discussed. The group would serve as a support mechanism for each person's career.

♦For the first year we would not address the *complicated salary review process.* The shareholders again met in January to establish salaries and agreed to revisit this issue later in the year.

Although the concepts developed by the Human Resources Team are sound, the implementation has been a disappointment. And I'm not quite sure how to solve it.

People are complaining about the absence of performance feedback--good or bad. The mentoring teams meet infrequently and when they do the interaction is sometimes ineffective.

For the past several months I have asked that discussion of someone else's performance not occur until the object of the discussion has received the feedback directly from the source. However, people continue to come to me with individual performance issues. I know this because I have tested each case that has come to me and seldom has the communication occurred. While I have suggested, and trust that, the communications occur immediately after our discussion, I have not attempted to "monitor" the follow-up.

What frightens me is the impact the negative discussions have on our organization, and especially on the younger associates. Some of this destructive conversation is entered into without malice, but it does not positively contribute to our efforts. It must stop. We owe this to each other.

During the past few months I have spent more time attempting to understand this issue than on client service. I believe the issue extends beyond the performance discussion.

I do not have an easy formula for addressing this problem.

I do not know whether this destructive behavior results from implementation shortcomings of the new system, or from individuals who do not share the firm's core value of open communication.

I have attempted to set the tone at the top by baring the soul of the firm through open book management and always being available to anyone who wants to talk with me. I am relying on the Human Resources Team with the support of the Noname Team to provide the leadership to achieve the desired level of communication.

Just because there are still problems does not mean we have failed. We will find a way.

Obviously, we have a way to go in this part of the reengineering effort. However, I have total confidence in the problem solving abilities of the process teams.

The Human Resources Team has already assumed responsibility for this important implementation issue and is taking steps necessary to improve our communication and feedback systems. By the next edition of this story the ***can do, will do*** attitude of ML&R will have prevailed and we will have a success story to tell. In the meantime, I have committed to telling our story, "warts and all."

In spite of challenges ahead, the Human Resources Team had considerable success in 1996. It revamped the entire salary review process and not only expanded the number of people involved in the salary administration process, but significantly improved the process of communicating salaries and performance expectations.

Another important achievement of the team was to develop and disseminate to the office a series of general performance expectations of our people. This is a remarkable document.

General Performance Expectations

from the Human Resources Team,
Maxwell Locke & Ritter

EVERYONE IN THE FIRM:

Everyone should embrace and live the firm's philosophy and its core values. That is why these values are on our walls, in the first chapter of the book, etc. We expect people to "talk the talk and walk the talk." In other words, everyone should assume personal responsibility for ensuring that their daily activities correspond to the strategies of their life and of the firm. Everyone should give serious attention to the annual commitment process and should use it as a tool to meet their individually defined goals and strategies.

Everyone should focus on becoming talented, balanced, quality-minded *people*, not just great *accountants or consultants.* The whole concept of the Atomic Model focuses on a pool of good *people* at the center. Without that, it will never work. We should want the right things...but for the right reasons, not necessarily because the boss expects it. If all of the expectations are met professionally, everyone is not necessarily any more balanced.

Although our expectations may seem overwhelming, we believe that "No success at work is worth failure at home." This is everyone's biggest challenge.

The expectations below assume a traditional career path. Those who choose a nontraditional career path must factor the relative amount of time they are working into the range of times shown below. Another thing to consider is that we have moved from an "up or out mentality" to one that allows people to stop at certain responsibility levels if they are contributing at that level and do not desire to move to the next level.

Zero to Two Years of Experience:

This is the most exciting period of public accounting in the sense that you begin to use your education. It is also a time when you will be exposed to more new information than during any previous two year period in your life.

Prepare to live to be 100! Many of you will. Adopt an attitude that supports life long learning. Never, never, never give up. Don't ever die before you're dead. Use every assignment, however dreadful it may seem, as a learning experience. Focus on what you are becoming, not on what you are doing.

Pass the CPA Exam.

Learn a core competency--either how to audit or how to prepare tax returns. Suit up and show up every day that health permits with a positive mental attitude. Do your best. Do the right thing and treat others the way you would like to be treated.

Adopt the philosophy that the only dumb question is the one you fail to ask. Actively seek performance feedback from your teachers. Clear your review notes on a timely basis. Offer to do more than you are asked. Spend time on your own to improve those skill sets that you believe are your weakest.

Improve your communications skills--the action plan will vary depending on the person, but the more one fears public speaking, the sooner one should decide to run toward that which is feared. Interact in team and client meetings, search for speaking engagements, teach a class at Langford or at the Austin Chapter, or join Toastmasters.

Begin a regular reading habit. This will enable you to stay current technically and more effectively communicate with your colleagues in client organizations. Five to seven hours of reading each week is probably the minimum required to accomplish this. Good sources include the daily paper; The Wall Street Journal; magazines such as Business Week, Money, Inc., Fortune; the Journal of Accountancy; business books; audit and tax alerts; information on the Internet; newsletters; industry journals; etc.

Attend a priority management class, buy an organizer (computer or manual) and develop this skill which will greatly improve your life and your potential.

Sharpen your PC skills. Push the envelope on the degree to which you use technology in your daily work.

Begin the business socialization process--participate in firm social events, firm community activities, etc.

Begin your business network by maintaining relationships with your former classmates, friends and neighbors.

Observe your in-charges so you can begin to borrow the traits that you believe will best fit the in-charge you wish to become. The sooner you act like an in-charge, the sooner someone will ask you to assume this role.

Do not take yourself too seriously.

THREE TO FIVE YEARS OF EXPERIENCE

This is the most challenging and stimulating period of your career because you wake up one day to the responsibility of being an in-charge accountant. The supervisory aspects of this challenge seem overwhelming. You are not sure of your own ability and suddenly you have responsibility for an entire engagement and two or three other people, who know less than you! You are beginning to sense that public accounting offers unlimited opportunities for personal sacrifice.

Build on all the above.

Develop in-charge skills--planning, organizing, teaching, supervising, leading, reviewing, interacting with clients, presentation skills--oral, graphic and written.

Move from a role of identifying issues to someone who analyzes, researches the situation and offers a range of acceptable solutions to the engagement team for discussion and approval.

Spend thirty minutes to an hour each day planning what your team members will do upon arrival. This can be done after everyone has left or before everyone gets to the job site. Review work each day. Do not wait until work is finished by your staff. Actively teach so that review notes are kept to a minimum. Those you write should be instructional and cleared by your staff before you hand the workpapers to a senior associate for review.

Focus on the accuracy of our reports--reference all numbers and statements of fact, *read and reread and reread our report drafts.*

Read the drafts aloud. You will be amazed how this will expose grammar and punctuation errors! Search for innovative ways to present our findings, industry trends, etc.

Begin a regular program of speaking to groups --teaching is an excellent forum, but there are others. Keep the client service team apprised of client related events, status of projects, etc. Search for ways to utilize technology to improve client related communications.

Approach your work as if you work for your client. This attitude increases your value to your clients and makes you more valuable to ML&R. You appreciate your clients and look forward to their calls. You enjoy working with them.

Finish what you start. See that work papers are filed within two weeks of completion of field work. Push the senior associate and shareholder to finish their part of this process.

Maintain contact with your clients throughout the year. Assume the role of convincing your clients of ways that either you or someone from the firm can help solve their business' problems. Work toward the goal of spending 25 percent of your time working on special projects. Take pride in having generated many of these projects.

Search for and assume leadership roles in ML&R process teams.

Assume the role of mentor to those with less experience.

SIX YEARS OF EXPERIENCE TO SHAREHOLDER ANNOUNCEMENT

This is by far the most rewarding, but at times the most frustrating of the various levels of public accounting. The frustrating part revolves around your assumption of total responsibility with no authority--at least in the contractual sense. The forces pulling at you are numerous and significant. At the same time, opportunities for personal sacrifice have grown geometrically since your in-charge days.

Build on all the above.

Manage and be accountable for client service delivery, client relations and extension of services to your clients. You are the person responsible for ensuring that services are delivered that meet or exceed our clients' expectations. When we fail to achieve this, you assume responsibility for appropriate communication with the client and implementing the follow-up necessary to salvage our client relationship.

Move from someone who analyzes and researches client situations to someone who is able to decide which of the acceptable alternatives best fits the client's situation. Then have the courage to make the decision.

Represent ML&R in leadership positions in the community. Nurture relationships that you established years ago. Establish confidence in your abilities so that your network begins to ask you to do work for their companies and their friends. Commit and deliver in such a way that you can attend any social function without the desire to avoid anyone in the room.

Supervision and review functions become assumed and you have grown into someone who is seen as a leader. By now you have assumed leadership roles internally and externally. Your actions clearly support the strategic directives of the firm.

Now, more than ever you work for your clients. You appreciate them as the people who pay for your children's food, clothes and college education. In addition, you are beginning to develop your own book of work. If you chose to leave the firm, this work would probably leave with you. You have become secure in the firm. You are not dependent on a shareholder retiring or other growth in the firm to secure ownership in the firm.

You are known as someone who is responsible for creating positive change, rather than someone who complains about things or serves as a barrier to change.

People join the firm, rather than leave, because of you. People look to you as a mentor. You have a skill set that allows you to assume a leadership role in virtually any project within the scope of your core competencies--the Atomic Model is your home.

The shareholders have confidence in your abilities and judgment to believe that in the near future you can be trusted to contractually obligate the firm--signing reports, tax returns, contracts, bank notes, etc.

When you have accomplished the above and people inside and outside the firm begin asking when you are going to make shareholder, or better yet, you are mistaken as a shareholder--you will be offered the opportunity.

SHAREHOLDERS

After a few months in this role, you realize that it is not the easy street you expected. However, you enjoy what you do and you look forward to what your work and relationships will become.

Our shareholders enjoy a comfortable standard of living, opportunities to participate in community and business-related board positions, and opportunities to speak, lecture and serve on various discussion panels. Shareholders are generally considered experts in their field and afforded the same civic respect as chief executive officers and owners of companies. The practice of public accounting provides an intellectually stimulating environment and allows for learning experiences in a wide variety of industries and situations, involving many business and community leaders. Shareholders also enjoy a flexible schedule which allows them to balance a wide variety of interests and priorities. Finally, shareholders enjoy the dynamics of being surrounded by a young and intelligent group of professionals.

A revised administrative manual, gender and other sensitive issues.

The Human Resources Team has completely revised the stakeholders' administrative manual, established an improved 401(k) plan, moved the office toward self-directed continuing professional education, and organized our first training sessions that addressed gender issues. We hired a well known expert in the area of gender issues. This decision more than paid for itself. With the expertise of an outside facilitator we were able to openly discuss difficult and sensitive gender issues. The discussions were long overdue and enabled us to take a significant step toward improving internal communication and healing deep-seeded, festering wounds. Some of the causes of the pain, resentment and anger cut to the core of our society and business culture. Others are products of having people under one roof who grew up in five entirely different decades--the thirties, forties, fifties, sixties and seventies.

Gender training: Is opening the doors to discussion asking for trouble?

I have mentioned to several other firms that we have recently participated in two sessions (eight hours) of gender training. Their response has been one of bewilderment. They ask why we would do such a thing. They ask what kind of a problem we had and how it surfaced. They ask if the training caused trouble by opening the door to this discussion. I can tell by their questions they either do not understand the issue or choose to ignore it. I suggest if they opened the doors to this discussion, they would be shocked by the firmly rooted gender differences that exist in their own firms. I am not sure they have agreed with me. A good reason to address gender issues is to take a giant step toward improving communication in the firm--and ultimately increasing productivity. At least this is our goal and we are moving toward it.

Soon we will benefit from learning about some of the same types of issues minorities deal with in the professional workplace. This will become increasingly important as we continue to hire minorities. Unlike the government plan, we will continue to implement an Equal Employment Opportunity Commission program that assures minorities the opportunity to succeed on their own, with the full support of our firm.

Where are we headed?

Our strategic focus is summarized as follows:

- **Improve one-on-one communications concerning performance and potential.**
- **Continue implementation of the Atomic Model.**

- **Proactively sell solutions driven services to existing clients.**
- **Maximize the use of technology.**
- **Develop emerging products and services.**
- **Implement officewide scheduling system.**

I have never been more confident in our ability to achieve these strategic initiatives.

Chapter 13: Increasing Profits Through the Atomic Model

◆ One foot into the new model, the other still entrenched in the pyramids ◆ Some bold steps out of our comfort zone ◆ How our old model worked ◆ The old model does not always provide the client value-added services ◆ Delivering client services as a circular instead of a linear model ◆ Out-sourcing for people with skill sets not within our firm ◆ Developing a seamless services model ◆ Redefined approach to client projects through the Atomic Model ◆ Eliminating or substantially reducing rework is an essential component ◆ Opportunity knocked: We were hired by a Fortune 500 company for a seemingly inconsequential consulting project ◆ In May, the Atomic Model was unveiled ◆ Once the Atomic Model is implemented, we expect our marketing efforts to skyrocket

By the fall of 1995, we realized the process teams were clearly functioning as teams. Although there were obstacles to overcome in achieving some of the team goals, the successful efforts were evident throughout the organization. The administrative efforts of the firm were thriving under the process teams. Prior to our move toward process teams, it was difficult to get any of our CPAs to do much of anything to support the administration of the office. However, during the past three years this situation actually *reversed* itself. Now, the CPAs seemed to prefer administrative assignments over client assignments. We began to understand that the attraction had more to do with the free flowing nature of the process teams than with the nature of the projects themselves.

Our recognition of this situation heightened when one of our top performers communicated his displeasure with his participation in client service delivery. We were surprised to learn that he was considering leaving the firm. He explained that, although the internal operations of the firm had been redefined, when he returned to the field to deliver services, he returned to the archaic service delivery model of the past.

We had failed to realize that our service delivery function remained deeply rooted in the hierarchy of the *pyramid* structure. In addition, communication barriers remained solid between the audit and tax disciplines. To further complicate the service delivery process, we were preparing to launch a consulting practice, to be announced in June 1996, as a separate division of Maxwell Locke & Ritter, p.c. While we prospered administratively, our client service functions were still burdened by pyramids.

To address this situation, we established a special task force to redefine our service delivery. We named this task force the Redefinition Team. In February 1996, in the midst of the traditional crisis-driven, stress-laden panic of a public accounting firm during its busy season, the Redefinition Team went to work. In an attempt to set the tone for anticipating the changes ahead, I had opened several meetings during the past three months with an overhead that read:

> **"If you're not living on the edge, you're taking up too much space."**
> *--Unknown*

We took some bold steps out of our comfort zone.

We chose the busiest time of the year to implement significant change because we convinced ourselves the best way to break a cycle is to interrupt it. This is exactly what we did--and did we ever!

The core team consisted of one shareholder and four senior associates--two each from the audit and tax disciplines--with a combined public accounting experience of over sixty years. Three of the members of this team were also significant contributors to the consulting practice being developed.

To effectively implement a process change as radical as the Atomic Model, we established a group of *experienced* people who were perceived by the rest of the organization to be "management."

We believed this was necessary to communicate to our office the message that the leadership of the organization was fully committed and believed the new model would work. We also recognized this team could not be successful without input from the entire organization. So, early on, we established that the core members of the Redefinition Team were its leadership, and every member of the firm was a member of this team who would be called upon at various stages of model development.

Until February, our framework for team management had been five separate teams linked together through the Noname Team. Each team had separate goals for development of its interests in the management of the firm. Team leaders reported the results and problems of team efforts to the Noname Team at scheduled meetings. Input from the Noname Team was then communicated to the process teams by the team leaders at their respective team meetings. We thought this was effective communication and the model depicted below was working.

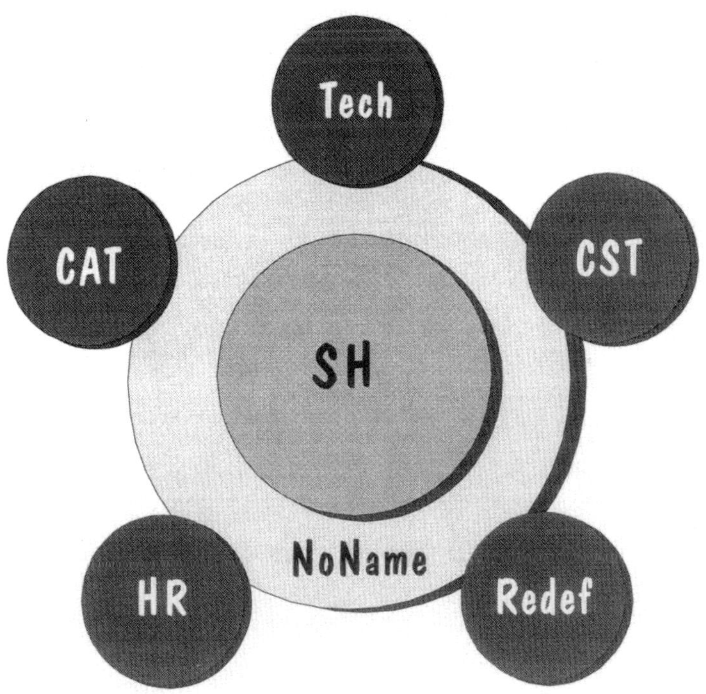

Once the Redefinition Team was in place, however, it did not take long to realize that the team's efforts were intertwined and the need to include considerations of all teams in team decisions was imperative. Communication had to improve. This realization allowed us to see that we had missed the point in designing our first circular model.

The model should really look like the target depicted below, the center of which should be our human resources.

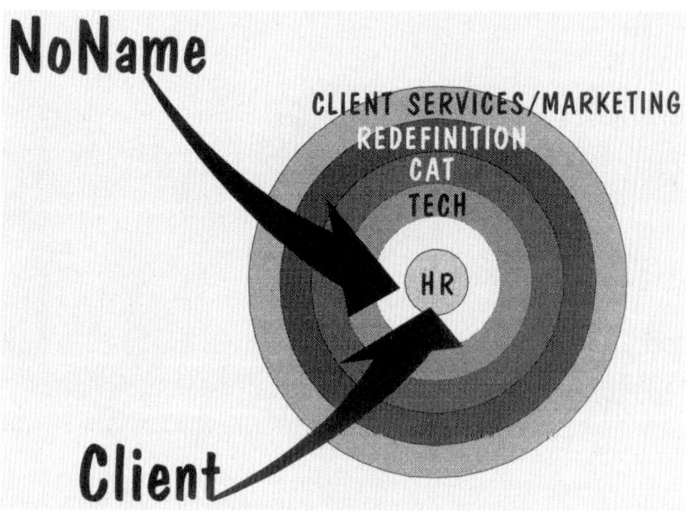

Once human resources are defined, the common area or place for work must be established. People must be provided with the technology necessary to do their job efficiently, a process must be in place to allow for effective use of resources, and the market must be defined and understood. The teams must work as a combined unit to create an environment focused on employee needs to allow each person to do their job successfully. If we could define such an administrative and operational process, we would become more profitable.

This sounded all too familiar. Five years before, our employees had arrived at the same conclusion in creating what became our philosophy statement, ***"We provide highest quality solutions and services from an environment which promotes each person's personal goals, self esteem and professionalism."***

Now, however, we had a culture that allowed the employees to participate freely in the development of the tool (or model) to accomplish the environmental (or internal) changes required. In order for you to understand the new model, I should first describe the old one.

In the traditional model of a public accounting firm, there is a hierarchy of individuals assigned to each client from the audit, tax and consulting disciplines. Each of these disciplines is organized in the shape of a pyramid, comprised of partners (twelve or more years of experience), senior managers (nine to twelve years), managers (six to nine years), seniors (three to six years), senior assistants (one to three years) and assistants (less than one year).

♦ People located toward the bottom of the pyramid perform much of the work, referred to as leveraging. About 80 percent of audit and tax work is performed by people with fewer than six years of experience.

♦ Analysis of the client's financial results and review of audit and tax fieldwork is performed by managers and partners.

♦ Within each departmental pyramid are many smaller pyramids along client service teams, industry teams and functional teams. These teams do not function in the circular fashion described herein. Rather, they function in the traditional hierarchical and linear manner.

The flow of information runs up and down the hierarchy of the audit group until completion of a report. The reports are presented to the client by upper level management of our firm at a meeting with the management, owners or board of the client.

It is unlikely for our staff--the people actually doing most of the work--to be engaged in conversation with the management, owner or board of the client. Rather, their communication efforts are with the controller and accounting personnel of the client.

Rarely does the accounting firm talk with the operations personnel of the client. As a result, many of our service providers know enough about the client to conduct an audit in accordance with professional standards and insert the numbers in the correct boxes on tax returns. However, they do not always know enough about the client's operations to carry on a meaningful conversation with the company's chief executive officer. Worse, the firm is not always positioned to provide value-added services to our clients.

Upon completion of the audit function, tax professionals retrieve audit files and reports and proceed with preparation of necessary tax returns. The move of the profession toward specialization in the seventies and eighties resulted in some interesting dynamics. Usually, little if any conversation occurs between the auditors and tax specialists. Before the audit report has been rendered or work on the tax return begun, the auditors have moved to another assignment and do not consider preparation of the client's tax returns to be their responsibility. Worse, many of our tax return preparers are not familiar enough with audit workpapers to effectively utilize them during the preparation of tax returns.

As amazing as this seems, the process begins all over again for tax work. The result is two independent processes with much rework involved within the second process.

Communication within the firm travels up and down the hierarchy of the tax group until completion of the tax returns for the client. The returns are often delivered by mail, delivery service or upper level management of the firm to the client. And again, often no communications between the people actually doing the work for the client occur with the owner or management of the client. Also, the owner or management of the client has individual tax returns which are not always prepared by the same group of tax professionals who prepare the company's tax return. In spite of this structure we provide a quality, historical document to our clients. We have done it for years.

The old model does not always provide the client value-added services.

However, our audit and tax teams do not always effectively provide value-added services and rarely have the knowledge to help our clients position themselves for the future. ***This is difficult for most CPAs to admit, but it is true.*** When a client desires such services, clients look to yet another group--the consulting department, and in many cases, another consulting firm--to provide important advice and perform special projects. In the national firm model, this group, often from out of town, usually works fairly independently of the auditors and tax accountants.

The success of our internally focused process teams had demonstrated to us that the traditional service delivery structure was an ineffective use of human resources. We recognized the creativity and talent which existed among the people comprising our own organization could benefit our clients, if we let it. So in February 1996, in the height of "busy" season, two mandatory meetings were called. The auditors first, and one week later, the tax professionals. The Redefinition Team leadership presented a new, somewhat undefined approach to service delivery, using the "target" theory.

We also introduced the idea of delivering client services as a circular instead of a linear model.

Those two presentations were nothing more than the introduction of an idea in its infancy, which, once planted, could be fostered to grow into a model for service delivery for all three disciplines--audit, tax and consulting. The initial vision for the process model included four phases of service delivery: planning, execution, delivery and acceptance/retention.

In each of these phases we planned to focus on human resources, both internally and externally. We recognized the need to have our clients involved in every step of the process. To effectively do this would require more than lip service to the almost worn out statement that "our people are our most important assets."

Finally, developing a circular model was a huge paradigm shift from the traditional one of distancing ourselves and our employees from the clients through limited, and sometimes restricted, communication efforts.

Our circular model involved the client in every step of the communications process.

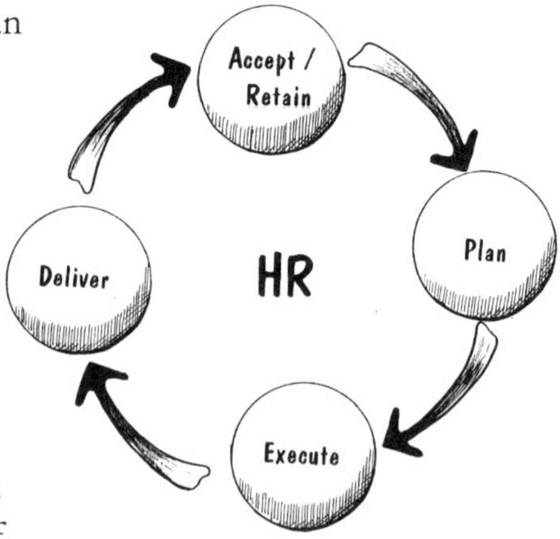

We recognized the potential need to outsource work which required skills we did not have. This, too, was a paradigm shift from the traditional approach to referring work toward working with other service providers on an engagement. The importance of providing value to our clients became the fundamental element driving this model. Understanding that people possess skill sets that enable them to provide quality services was paramount to the success of this process. We recognized that each individual within an organization contributes to the success of that organization. We envisioned using the various skills held by members of our own firm to enhance the ability to assist our clients in conducting their businesses. In short, people at all experience levels of our firm could add value to the services provided our clients, if given the opportunity. The process model had to allow flexibility in the human resources element as well as open communication among the entire team, including the client.

According to the model, each phase of the process is examined independently on each project to determine the most effective use of resources to provide quality service. For each phase we consider:

Human Resources: Who should the team for this phase include to best serve this client?

Common Area: What is the best location for this phase of the process to be conducted?

Technology: What technology should be used?

Client Service: What approach to value-added service should we take for this client?

Developing a seamless services model.

The initial model suggests the steps involved in each phase. Consideration of these steps, along with available resources allow the team to develop and maintain a long term relationship with a client, which results in seamless services. Client service should be provided throughout the year, not once a year or when there is a problem. We want our model to allow for continuous client interaction. Therefore, the phases of the engagement have become fluid. We knew this would eventually occur, but we had to jump start it somehow. So, we developed a guide, designed to be redesigned, redesigned, and redesigned again.

The proposed planning phase of a project includes information gathering, risk assessment, development of the approach for execution and communication of expectations of the team and the individual team members. The client is included in the planning phase, a situation which has only occurred on a limited basis in the past. We have tested the concept of including clients in the planning phase of our engagements and have had positive responses. They welcome the open communication with all people involved. Most important, the new model focuses on the critical need to include the ***entire*** service team--auditors, tax specialists, young and old.

1. Plan

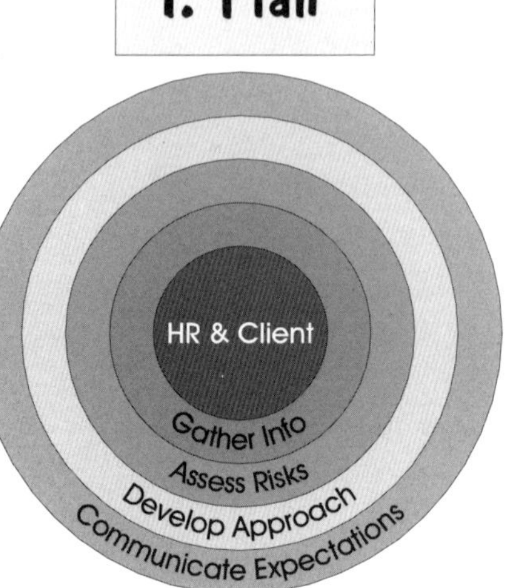

2. Execute

The execution phase includes investigation of information, resolution of issues, documentation of findings and preparation of reports, if applicable.

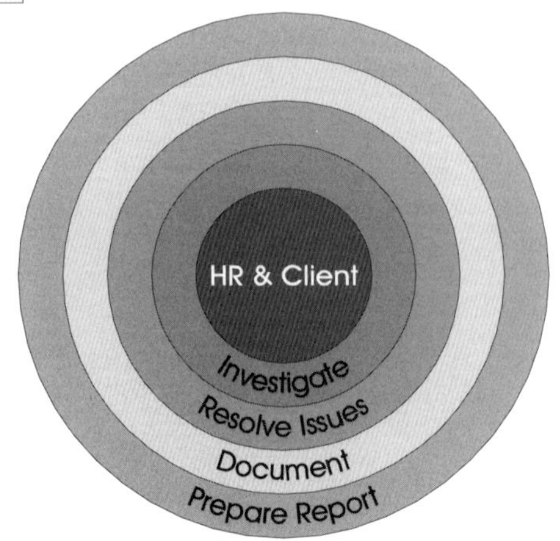

3. Deliver

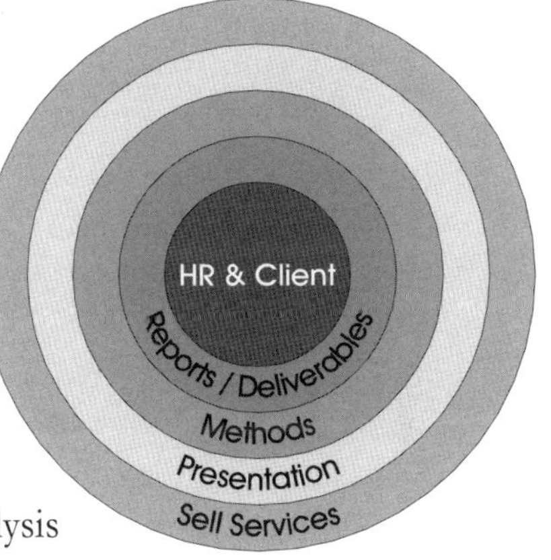

The delivery phase considerations include the deliverables (reports, tax returns, flow charts, etc.), the method of delivery, preparation of presentation and analysis of client needs for further services.

4. Accept/ Retain

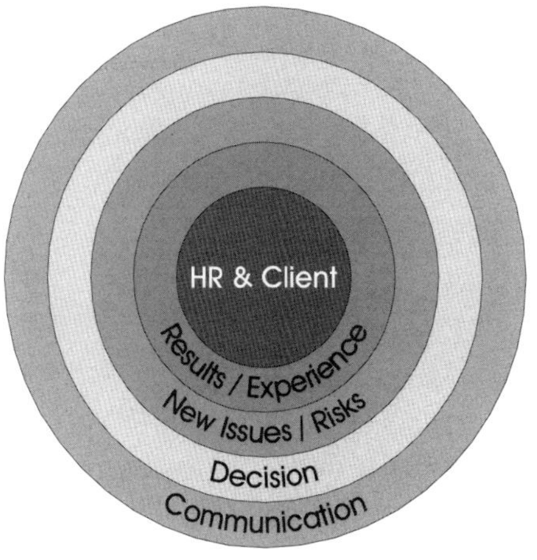

The accept/retain phase of the project follows every delivery. The team reviews the results and experiences relating to the client and discusses issues or risks that jeopardize the client relationship. Following these discussions, a decision concerning the continuation of the relationship is made and communicated to the client.

The process model incorporates a dynamic team concept which approaches project design with an *operations focus.* This allows the team to focus on issues early enough in the process to be effective contributors to client decisions, targeting issues rather than habits and gaining an improved understanding of the client's business. The team approach improves efficiency by eliminating rework and other unnecessary steps in the project process. It also allows younger professionals to be exposed to business decisions and project considerations. This enhances their understanding of the jobs they are performing, accelerates the training process, and provides an environment in which inexperienced professionals learn and contribute their skills as team members. It is not uncommon for creative ideas to develop from a question asked by the most inexperienced team member. At the same time, inexperienced team members are exposed to input from more experienced people, thereby speeding the learning curve.

Once again, these dynamics only occur if the entire client service team meets during critical junctures of the client service process. As we have plotted the new approach, we have found that regularly getting the entire client service team together is a challenge. However, we are committed to overcoming this challenge.

What have we learned during early implementation of these models?

As mentioned earlier, many of our clients require audit and tax services which we formerly approached almost as if they were independent projects. Audits were conducted by completing a series of linear tasks presented to the auditors in the form of audit programs. Audit tasks were assigned to auditors based on complexity and experience levels of team members. Less experienced staff members were not involved in the planning, delivery or client acceptance/ retention phases; their participation was limited to execution. Their role was "tick and tie, do or die." Worse, shareholders rarely participated in the planning or execution phases in a meaningful way. A similar, but relatively independent approach was used to prepare the client's tax returns.

Under what we now call the Atomic Model, completion of the audit, tax returns, and special projects is approached as one process. The entire audit team begins to approach an audit as a process rather than as a series of audit steps. *All* audit team members participate in the four phases of the audit process. Emphasis is placed on planning the audit process with the goal of eliminating rework during the execution and delivery phases.

Eliminating or substantially reducing rework is an essential component of the new model.

This represents our first serious attempt to prevent spending the last 20 percent of the audit on what we now understand to be rework. Members of the tax team periodically participate in the audit process, enabling the entire client service team to gain a better knowledge of client needs. With proper planning and communication between audit and tax specialists, much of the information necessary for preparation of tax returns is gathered during the audit process.

What a novel thought!

During the course of client service delivery, the cross functional team meets on several occasions. The dynamics of these team meetings are fascinating. With the new model, wonder of all wonders, the less experienced staff have much to offer!

More importantly, they are exposed to all aspects of our project and learn more quickly. I believe three years of participating in this model will produce learning for inexperienced staff that would have taken five years under the traditional "tick and tie" model. Finally, the client benefits through our more efficient client service delivery, enhanced ability to provide value-added services and a greater number of knowledgeable service providers.

During the two February meetings, the Redefinition Team requested input from the firm and asked the group to change their approach. Two client teams adopted the model between February and April.

Quarterly, we heard from those two teams which have grappled with the new model.

While the reports were far from glowing, the consensus was unanimous: *Continue this approach. It will work--eventually. We need tools to make it happen. Give us some guidance. Let us keep refining and improving the process.*

The model was in its infancy in February when it was introduced. Between February and May, the team leadership wrestled with the various factors surrounding the process model.

The question was, what does Maxwell Locke & Ritter look like, using this approach to service delivery? The team knew we were not a pyramid. They also recognized we were attempting to break down the communication barriers between audit and tax functions.

Still, no one was sure exactly how to do this.

Opportunity presented itself when we were hired by a Fortune 500 company to do one project.

"Large oak trees grow from small acorns." Soon the lone project became five consecutive projects over an eight month period. These projects were led by the two senior associates involved in leading the Redefinition Team. Together they actively staffed these projects

with people from our traditional disciplines--audit, tax and administration.

The results were obvious. These people began to interact. Discussions about the new approach to service delivery were continuous and by May the team leadership had developed the Atomic Model. Another important part of the project was that our people were exposed to a large company that operated under many of the free flowing concepts of the Atomic Model.

Our relationship with the Fortune 500 client continues and we value the opportunity to serve this company.

The *Atomic Model* is a series of diamonds fanned into a circular shape, the center of each resting at the same point. The points of the diamonds represent skill sets either now existing or being developed through education or strategic alliance. In the center of the diamonds are our human resources and their core competencies, surrounded by the process model.

The diamond shape is not used by coincidence.

Currently, if you look at the experience levels of the complement of people now representing the firm work force, we are in a diamond shape. The far sides of the diamond repre-

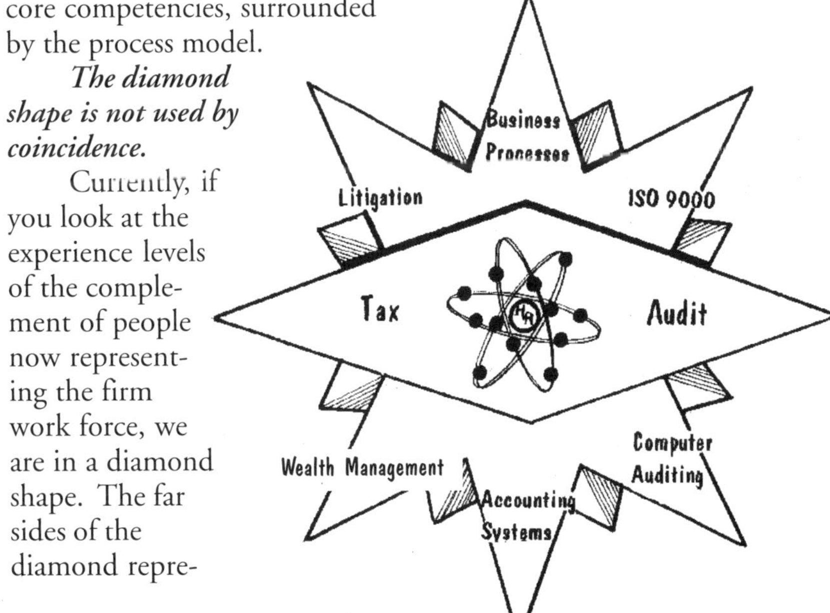

sent the audit and tax functions.

We turned the two pyramids ninety degrees and merged them, creating a common pool of human resources.

Keeping in mind that people have different skill sets and that our objective was to increase the consulting efforts of the firm, we recognized that audit and tax services are not our only niches. As a matter of fact, we fully expect these two "cash cows" will diminish in the next few years, and we are planning for that change. In the meantime, we intend to continue delivering quality core services while positioning ourselves for the future.

Therefore, our people will be expected to develop core competencies in either audit or tax, while expanding their horizons by participating in specialized consulting projects. The spikes in the model, which represent consulting niches, will be fluid and we expect that they will change more frequently in the future as product lives and attention spans continue to shorten.

The Atomic Model clearly positions us for the impact of the statement I recently read, which encourages us to build a *skills inventory. Five years from today, fully one-third to one-half or greater of your firm's revenues will come from providing services that you do not now provide.*

This was far beyond the norm for an accounting firm and it took some analysis and evaluation for people first to understand and then believe in the model.

The Redefinition Team leadership recognized this obstacle and, the following month, launched a program to make it happen. The team presented a list of approximately thirty projects to be completed by the end of 1996, including:

♦ Define and document the four phases of the process model (create the tools requested in May)

♦ Revise the scheduling system (imperative under the new model)

♦ Provide marketing training (leveraging skill set marketing to the entire firm), time management training (personal responsibility), and interview skills development (information gathering).

The majority of projects on the list were born of necessity to force the new model to work. The list was presented, prioritized by the members of the firm, and scheduled for completion. Participation on any project team was voluntary, but the response of firm members was significant.

The first meetings of the project teams were scheduled and two weeks later the team leaders, selected at the initial meeting, reported to the group meeting. Once a month we met with Karl Krumm in an office wide session and project team reports were made to the entire office. Karl's role at these monthly meetings was to help us change from the traditional audit/tax mentality to one of becoming our client's preferred business advisor.

We need to think of ourselves based upon our many and diverse skill sets, rather than upon our traditional audit/tax roles. Once we conquer this obstacle and have the Atomic Model better defined and better tooled, we can expect our marketing efforts to ***skyrocket.***

When the entire team is armed with client knowledge and each individual is allowed to freely discuss ideas for improvement with the team, the ability of the firm to add value to client service is expanded. This effort, coupled with the improved efficiencies expected of the process model, can only produce increased profitability for M L& R.

How do we quantify this?

We cannot, at least not yet.

But, based on what we have experienced over the past three years, we believe the Atomic Model was beginning to work before we understood how to draw it.

We do know that the financial statements of the firm for 1996 reflect twice the amount of consulting revenues and five times the 1991 amount.

Chapter 14: The Future-- Public Accounting 2010

♦ Let's pretend we are already living in 2010 ♦ The nature of financial statement audits has entirely changed ♦ We introduce ourselves not as CPAs, but as information brokers ♦ Sources of revenues in the year 2010 look like this ♦ Between 1996 and 2010, many organizations failed ♦ Important words like *location, location, location* are replaced by *technology, technology, technology* ♦ Our use of electronic media has eliminated the need for file and mail rooms ♦ Business travel has almost become a thing of the past ♦ Although there is less personal interaction with colleagues, we keep up with each other electronically ♦ Sabbaticals have become a fringe benefit

---

What will the future hold for public accounting firms?

By the Year 2010, I believe our profession will not even resemble what it looked like for most of the twentieth century. The major trends that will affect our profession are organized along the following lines:

- **Services provided**
- **Competition**
- **Technology**
- **Human resources**
- **Globalization**

My ideas have not been formulated through research, think tanks, focus groups or surveys. They are just my thoughts. My only qualification as a futurist is that I have taken a few hours to write these thoughts in this book. As a matter of fact, until a few months ago I had never seriously considered writing a book. If my thoughts on the future of the accounting profession have any value, it may be that they have been the foundation for the recent changes in our firm.

Let's pretend we are already living in 2010.

Services Provided

In 1996, I kept telling our people that by the year 2000, over half of our revenues would be generated by services we did not currently perform. Now, it is ***2010***, and our revenue sources do not even slightly resemble those of 1996.

Major changes have occurred in the U.S. tax code, which now resembles a hybrid of the ***flat tax***, a ***national sales tax*** and a ***value added tax***. The ten year transition period between the old and new tax systems has been completed. This transition period provided us some consulting opportunities and it allowed us to continue performing some compliance services as the former system was being phased out.

Depreciation, charitable contributions, tax exempt income and mortgage interest were some of the last components of the old system to die. This change in the tax code, coupled with the tax reporting software that has become so common, has all but eliminated the tax compliance and tax consulting services that provided 50 percent of our total revenues in 1996.

Some of this income has been replaced with that generated by the government's requirement that all corporate tax remissions be audited by an independent accountant. Newt Gingrich and the Republican Congress of the late nineties borrowed this concept from the rest of the industrialized world. Independent audits of tax returns had been their practice for many years. By the way, all tax remissions including the necessary supporting documentation are ***electronically filed***.

The nature of financial statement audits has entirely changed. Bean counting is a lost art.

In the past, we performed an audit of historical information. Audit reports were usually rendered two to six months after the end of the year we had examined. This made some of the information

reported as much as eighteen months old. Auditors practically lived in the past.

Now, the world has been linked by a huge communication system, effectively creating a world of ***on-line information***. In financial arenas, today's information is immediately available to stockholders, Wall Street analysts, lenders, suppliers, customers, competitors, employees, governments, news media, and anyone else who is interested in it.

Reflecting the on-line nature of the world, ***we are electronically linked with our clients.*** We perform daily tests of their internal control systems, and much of our testing is done through the computer. It is important to those who access on-line information, that the data be reliable. Each day we deliver an independent auditors' report on the ***reliability*** of the system that is producing that day's information and our report appears on the ***Internet***. Running the necessary tests of the internal control system normally takes about thirty minutes per day. At the end of our clients' fiscal years, we perform some extended procedures, the results of which are reported on the Internet within five business days of fiscal year end.

We introduce ourselves not as CPAs, but as information brokers.

Our largest revenue source has become searching for and sifting through the infinite amounts of information available to our clients.

Clients find it more cost-effective to out-source the information analysis to us. We provide a service that helps them better run their businesses.

In addition to analyzing information for the benefit of our clients, we have become the primary financial forecasters and economists in the business world. As the world has become a myriad of choices, we have taken on the necessary task of sifting through thousands of factors that surround each strategic business decision and presenting our clients three or four choices from which to choose. We base our reputation in the business community on providing clients not only with a variety of options but also ***with the confidence that they have the tools to make sound business decisions.***

We are paid handsomely for these services. Actually, justifying our bills is easier now than it was in "the good old days." Back then, our work was viewed either as a necessary evil or as a commodity that kept our clients out of trouble with the IRS. Now, our work focuses on the future and allows our clients to remain competitive in a rapidly changing marketplace. Our service mix has also changed.

Sources of revenues in the year 2010 look like this:

♦ **Audits of corporate tax remissions**	**15 %**
♦ **Audits of on-line information systems**	**15 %**
♦ **Analysis of information, strategic planning and forecasting**	**50 %**
♦ **Niche business consulting services**	**20 %**

COMPETITION

Our competition bears little resemblance to that of 1996. The Big Six firms and the two national firms have combined. These firms, along with a large financial services firm have become the Big Four.

Several international strategic alliances of local firms effectively compete with the Big Four, and small independent tax firms have almost become a thing of the past. The accounting and tax return preparation services that previously supported these firms are no longer necessary. Many independent CPAs practice in small niche consulting firms. Even more people work as individuals, often linking with other individuals and groups to perform certain projects. With the exception of the period before the industrial revolution, there are more small businesses than any other time in history.

In addition to the Big Four, competition has extended to the other major players in the financial services industry. The regulatory barriers to competition, once protected by the State Board of Public Accountancy, have been declared unconstitutional. The CPA designation continues to command some respect in the attest function that provides about 30 percent of our revenue. However, in the other service areas we compete with other financial service firms in a no holds barred environment. To position ourselves, our strategic alliance of local CPA firms has partnered with several of these competitors in well-defined relationships to further the interests of both parties. On a local basis, we have done the same with several other service providers.

Technology and Human Resources

Prior to the 1800s, commerce followed shipping lanes and rivers. From the 1800s through the mid-1900s, commerce shifted to the rail lines and later to a farm to market road system. From the mid-1900s to 2000, commerce moved to the interstate highway system and ultimately the airport system.

With each shift in commerce, towns and cities died when they could not or chose not to move to the newest transportation system depot. By the early 2000s, the same thing happened to about 25 percent of the companies and organizations that failed to understand the impact the Internet would have on commerce.

They did not die because goods and people were moving differently. They died because ***the Internet forever changed the paths of information and resulting commerce.*** Other organizations died because the technology revolution of the nineties resulted in a consumer revolution that demanded speed and quality of service the organizations could not provide.

Between 1997 and 2010, many organizations failed.

The failure resulted from two primary factors: first, they could not keep pace with the changing technologies, the resulting products (product cycles shrunk from eighteen months in 1996 to six weeks today) and operating efficiencies; and second, they could not motivate their workforces toward the innovation necessary to keep pace with the rapid rate of change driven by technology. Most organizations survived until the early 2000s, but eventually found themselves in a *Catch-22* situation similar to what Joseph Heller (one of my favorite authors during my young adult years) described in his novel.

Important words like location, location, location are replaced by technology, technology, technology!

New technologies have made it possible for our associates to work from remote locations. All of our associates have a home office that is furnished by the firm. This proved cost effective because it reduced our need for office space by 60 percent. Although we provide the furniture and equipment, we do not pay rent for space in people's homes. However, we are beginning to receive some pressure from Generation Z to provide this as a fringe benefit.

Our use of electronic media has eliminated the need for file and mail rooms.

Indeed, we have no walls at all, except for our four conference rooms. Our office is organized so teams of three or four people can work most effectively in ***project teams.*** We have moved from the "hotel" to the "motel" concept--one closer to the idea of a Motel 6 than a Hyatt Regency.

Actually it more closely resembles a nice KOA Campground. After a stay in the campground, people break camp and leave their campsite cleaner than they found it. We have a campground host who mediates campsite disputes and generally makes the camper's stay enjoyable.

Most meetings in our office are scheduled either early or late in the business day so children can be transported to or from the preschool located on the first floor of our building. Children of our firm have access to a ML&R scholarship fund for post-high school technical training or college tuition.

Business travel has almost become a thing of the past.

It has been replaced by various communication systems, including video conferencing equipment and a ***virtual reality*** system that allows us to step into the meeting room without leaving the workplace. Most technology systems are voice driven. My grandchildren do not know the meaning of DOS or Windows. My children describe the technology of the eighties and nineties to their children using the same techniques I once used to describe the drive-in movies of the sixties to them.

Although there is less personal interaction with colleagues, we keep up with each other electronically.

We begin each week with a gathering in the office even though we could do it electronically. This forces the social interaction human beings still require. We have placed more emphasis on social and family gatherings.

Discussions of spirituality in the workplace have been introduced to our office as an integral part of our wellness programs. Although the former shareholders of the firm (trustees of the ESOP) continue to draw salaries, everyone else in the firm is an independent contractor. Many of these contractors own stock in the firm through the ML&R Employees' Stock Ownership Plan. The contractors are paid by the project.

We still have a time reporting system, but it is used as a cost accounting system rather than as a revenue system.

We no longer bill by the hour, but by the project or the procedure performed. Our clients ***love*** this. Under the old system they never believed any accounting function could take as long as it did and always believed our rates were exorbitant.

Public accounting firms no longer provide the training ground for the corporate world's accountants and finance officers. Now the model is reversed. Upon graduating from a five or six year university accounting program, graduates accept positions with accounting or finance departments of Fortune 500 companies. These graduates have better communication, interpersonal, analysis, problem solving, innovative thinking and multidisciplinary skills than did graduates of fifteen years ago. After five years or so many people leave those companies to join financial service firms. They bring to us a significant industry or functional skill set that can be applied directly to our clients' needs. Our training programs assume basic technical skills and now focus on service development and changing technologies.

Sabbaticals have become a fringe benefit.

Although the terms of these sabbaticals vary, our firm offers a sabbatical to members who have at least five years of continuous service.

Every five years each person is required to separate themselves from firm related work for a continuous period of seven to eight weeks.

The sabbatical is four weeks plus the normal vacation period. Voice mail and e-mail are routed to other individuals. The person is restricted from access to our Internet during the sabbatical. Some people take extended vacation trips. Others enroll in intensive summer school college courses. A few spend time at home relaxing and doing household projects.

We have found the benefits of these sabbaticals to be significant. People return with a refreshed outlook and sometimes a new or improved skill set.

Globalization

Technology has made the world a much smaller place. We do not physically have to be in Singapore or Buenos Aires to meet with national or international clients. Now we are electronically linked by sight, sound, feeling and smell. These communication advances mean everyone--not just the former Big Six firms--can do business internationally.

Knowledge of international business, accounting practices and cultures is mandatory.

Our affiliation of local firms provides us with the necessary languages to serve many of our international clients. In our local office we have people who converse in Spanish, Japanese, Chinese and Korean. Spanish is required by most of our clients who do business in Latin America. This need has been met by the one third of our work force that is Hispanic.

Finding a workforce able to speak the key languages of the Pacific Rim has been more difficult, but we met this need because of the Pacific Rim linkages of our high tech clients.

One fourth of our workforce is African-American.

Our firm now qualifies as a historically underutilized business--although this term has not been used for over ten years. ***Over half of the firm is owned by women, minorities and people who speak English as a second language.***

Chapter 15: Things to Consider Before You Begin

♦ Why this book was written ♦ Before you attempt to move in this new and exciting direction, please read the following ♦ You do not have to throw the baby out with the bath water ♦ Creativity is essential in preparing your firm for the future ♦ The importance of being earnest, and still having having fun ♦ The importance of focusing on things which are really important

---

Initially, this book was written to provide an orientation to people who have recently joined our firm or who will join us in the future.

The more we reengineer and the larger we grow, fewer people will have been with us long enough to have insights into our transformation.

Why this book was written.

Several people, outside our firm, encouraged me to write the history of our firm. The story has been difficult to communicate in soundbites during our periodic office meetings, and many of our colleagues in other firms who hear the soundbites think we are absolutely crazy. So I am sure that some of the people who have recently joined our firm think so, too. For the people who have lived the story, the frequent soundbites are a bit repetitious.

I committed to developing an orientation course for people new to our firm. This book is a part of that effort. What began as a two or three page overview expanded into what you have just read.

This book will be read by people who join our firm. Upon joining us, they will attend an orientation session where concepts described in the book will be discussed and questions answered. We hope this approach speeds the assimilation process for new people.

Although the book was conceived as an orientation tool, it is ultimately intended for leaders of professional service firms who are already convinced of the need to redefine their own firms.

I hope you will consider this new approach to managing or, better yet, leading a professional service firm.

Stop! Before you attempt to move in this new and exciting direction, please read the following:

1. Commitment

The managing shareholder of the firm must be convinced of the new approach and absolutely committed to the conversion process. Implementing the concepts discussed in this book have been the most difficult thing I have done in my adult life. The cultural changes required of this new approach have taken longer and met more resistance than I imagined. This change in your business culture will probably need to be in effect for three to five years before you begin to recognize tangible results. When asked how often I thought about abandoning the new approach, I respond, "about every two or three months" and smile. Truthfully, during the transition you will often take two steps forward and one step back. Although progress continues, you may frequently disappoint yourself by reverting to old ways and others will disappoint you, too. Do not attempt this journey unless you are willing to accept the *toughest* leadership assignment in your corporate life. Keep in mind, however, that the results can also be the most rewarding of your career.

2. Support

Once you are ready to accept the challenge, do not attempt this until you have an appropriate level of support from your fellow shareholders or partners. Do not expect a consensus. More than likely, you will not get it. You must have a majority of partners who are convinced to the point of advocating the required systemic changes. From those who are not convinced you must obtain a commitment not to sabotage or undermine the reengineering efforts. Seemingly innocent comments, jokes and ridicule may constitute sabotage and cannot be tolerated. The leader must be assertive enough to squash this behavior as it comes to his or her attention. This is one exception to moving away from the use of fear as a motivator, which is advocated in this book. Your partners must understand that you are so committed to these changes *you will not tolerate* any behavior that contradicts the new direction of the firm.

3. Casualties

Be prepared for and willing to accept personnel casualties. Not everyone in your organization will be willing or able to change. Most of these people will leave the firm within two years of the beginning of the reengineering effort. Another group will be stretched to their limits to make the necessary changes to their habits. Fortunately, a third group will embrace the exciting new direction and become advocates of reengineering. I was surprised that the largest number of casualties came from our ranks of mid-managers. These were people who had five to ten years (28 to 35 years old) invested in the traditional model and may have experienced difficulty accepting that the old promises were being pulled away from them. These people expected to work hard for a period of time and at some point to have the trappings of success--window office, status, secretary, four weeks vacation, club membership, security and a salary of six digits or more. Also, they looked forward to achieving the level at which someone else would do most of their work for them. As managers, they could put the same pressures on associates that their managers had put on them, and they could blame associates for any work of less than standard quality.

4. Outside Help

Do not be surprised if you require outside assistance. We almost abandoned the idea of this new approach after two years of attempting it on our own. The introduction of an organizational consultant saved our effort. His knowledge and expertise enabled us to move from dead center and significantly increase our progress. For me, it reduced to an acceptable level, the tremendous pressures that seemed to be concentrated on me. As we worked with the consultant, behavior that reverted to our old ways was met with the reminder, "What would Karl say about what we are about to do?" The ability to deflect some of the responsibility to an independent party was very important. Also, the independent third party received more attention and respect than we would have given each other. This credibility elevated the importance of the effort among our own people and reinforced our efforts. As a result, the progress of our reengineering increased *rapidly* after the introduction of an independent influence.

5. Piecemealing won't work

Do not attempt to piecemeal certain aspects of this approach. Open book management concepts, participatory decision making, profit sharing, mentoring teams, process teams, the cross generational and functional leadership team, and redefinition of client service delivery model are each dangerous to implement on a case by case basis because many of these concepts build on each other. As a whole, they work well together and complement each other; however, on a piecemeal basis they may cause chaos. The turmoil may require you to adopt a concept you would rather not use, or worse, revert to the old way of operating. Most of these concepts require systemic change in your business culture. You must decide either to take the plunge or to stay in your comfort zone. Without total commitment, a slow death would be easier than the confusion and bedlam caused by a haphazard approach to reengineering.

You do not have to throw the baby out with the bath water.

Some of the concepts discussed in this book can be applied to the traditionally managed professional service firm. Examples of these include group development of the mission statement, core values, and strategies of the firm. Maximizing efforts of the emerging work force, development of family friendly policies, commitment to the community and establishment of strategic alliances are other examples of changes that can be made on a case by case basis without committing to a significant reengineering effort.

I believe those firms who ignore the massive changes that are affecting them will ***wither*** over the next several years. There are two primary forces driving my belief. First, the traditionally managed firm will not keep pace with the rapid rate of change that will occur in the future; and second, the traditionally managed firm will not be able to attract and retain the best professionals.

However, I am convinced the approach outlined in this book will enable you to position your firm for a better future. I believe this approach will enable your firm to foster an environment that encourages creativity and innovation.

Creativity is essential in preparing your firm for the future.

Creativity is absolutely essential in preparing a new approach for your firm--one which recognizes that people are no longer motivated to the extent once thought by money and security. Instead, the emerging workforce is motivated by the need for respect as individuals, interesting and challenging work, and a desire for recognition of their efforts. The concepts discussed in this book support the needs of the emerging workforce.

The importance of being earnest, and still having fun.

Much has changed in the twenty years that I have practiced public accounting. In the traditional CPA firm, work was not supposed to be fun. Laughter often evoked a verbal reminder that the job was to do work, not to have fun.

The new approach enables even a stodgy old CPA firm to create and sustain an enjoyable, caring, family sensitive and productive environment, because it:

♦ Encourages honesty, dignity and respect in the conduct of all business matters;

♦ Reinforces the importance of the human side of our business;

♦ Produces an environment that encourages people to hit the numbers that are very black and white, in a workplace where people have a greater ability to relax than they had in the former stressful environment;

♦ Creates an environment that encourages a sense of community within the workplace and provides people the support necessary to succeed in our complex times;

♦ Provides people more than just a place to perform audits, prepare tax returns and pick up a paycheck;

♦ Encourages people to seek purpose and meaning in their lives.

The importance of focusing on things which are really important.

We have found that living our core values helps us develop healthy and balanced long-term relationships with our customers. By striving to keep our families foremost, we become better performers in our business. By giving unselfishly to our community, we become infused with a deep sense of satisfaction and gratitude. We have found a means of realistically building each person's self esteem and integrity.

The result is a happier workforce and a more productive firm. This is excellent motivation to endure the pain of cultural transformation described in this book.

Most important, it is the right thing to do!

Summary: Service, Prosperity and Sanity

In summary, the new approach described in this book can enhance your firm's ability to provide quality ***service*** to your clients, while creating a new kind of ***prosperity*** and maintaining ***sanity*** among the members of your firm. I believe this is what most professional service firms are seeking. In any event, the thesis supports the title of my first book. Now, I will return to the accounting and consulting practice I love, and to the people with whom I love to work.

Thank you to all who have contributed to the efforts described in this book.

I hope everyone enjoyed the story.

Good luck on your journey and Godspeed to you!

Epilogue: My Return from Vacation

♦ The first three meetings dealt with dissatisfaction and negative attitudes in the office ♦ To put it mildly, things were stacking up ♦ By Wednesday, I was ready to abandon our reengineering efforts and sell the firm ♦ Things seemed impossible but the new system worked and everything got done ♦ Five years ago, the story would have been quite different ♦ Yes, there was dissatisfaction and some negatives to face. So what! Nobody's perfect ♦ I will return to the office with a heightened appreciation for difficulties caused by change

---

I returned to the office after a two week vacation which had been planned for months. I managed to go for two weeks without listening to voice mail, calling the office, having the office call me, or using my laptop. I did not answer a phone or even look at my organizer. This says a lot for someone who relies on his organizer. I had been out of town for three of the past four weeks; and quite frankly, it felt as if I had been gone for the entire month. My return was most interesting. Reflections on surviving that first week back in the office, gave birth to this Epilogue.

I was told that an epilogue is the place where an author writes a commentary on the commentary already presented. My time away from the office allowed me to see changes in the office a bit differently upon my return and caused me to pause and ponder. In short, my return to the office furnished plenty of fodder for a commentary.

The first three meetings dealt with dissatisfaction and negative attitudes in the office.

People are not happy, I was told. The reasons for the dissatisfaction were as varied as the people who explained them.

Some thought the root causes were resistance to changes occurring as a result of implementing the Atomic Model. Others thought the changes were not occurring fast enough.

Some blamed it on negative people or "bad" people. Others blamed it on people who wear rose-colored glasses in the office and are oblivious to problems.

Some believed this "reengineering jazz" established unrealistic expectations regarding workloads, balance and quality of life--goals that can never be achieved by a professional services firm. Others disagreed with this.

Some blamed it on a rapidity of growth in the firm that most people have not experienced. Others blamed it on the nature of the growth--consulting is "too unpredictable and requires a lot of thinking."

Some blamed it on those people who have taken on responsibilities they are not capable of handling. Others blamed it on the unwillingness of some to accept responsibility for the dynamic organization we had become.

Some blamed it on the inexperience of a staff that requires too much supervision. Others thought we were understaffed and lacked people to whom we could delegate work.

No one blamed it on record profits and the first *midyear* profit sharing distribution ($63,000) in our history.

To put it mildly, things were stacking up...on me!

While I was participating in these discussions, one of our key people had an apparent heart attack and spent four days in the hospital to determine the source of chest pains.

I had numerous phone calls to return and the phone continued to ring.

I had fifteen meetings scheduled for the week.

One client was in final negotiations for the sale of a several million dollar business and required much assistance from our firm. This situation required serious overtime and resulted in childcare issues for one of our young working mothers.

On the second day of my return, we received within ten minutes two phone calls from clients requiring significant assistance from us before the end of the week. We had no one immediately available, but expressed confidence in our ability to respond to their emergencies.

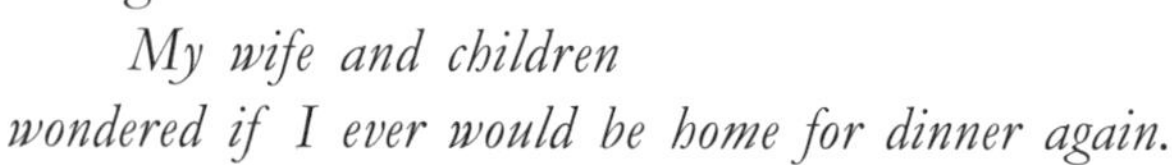

My wife and children wondered if I ever would be home for dinner again.

A local newspaper reporter desperately needed an interview with me in order to finish his story for the Sunday edition.

The community college's presidential search committee that I co-chaired required my immediate attention.

Another nonprofit organization wanted to know when I would get around to making the necessary phone calls to sell sponsorships to their golf tournament.

The battery in my car died.

A city councilman needed to talk with me.

My parents wondered why I had not called since returning from vacation.

I met with two prospective clients who had heard great things about our firm. I tried to appear calmer than I really was.

The ultimate insult was a voice mail I sent the entire office on Thursday. I admitted I had not managed my time well enough to prepare for a time management course I was scheduled to teach the next day.

On Wednesday evening, I was ready to abandon our reengineering efforts and sell the firm.

As it turned out, the chest pains endured by my friend and colleague *were not* the result of a heart attack.

I returned all of my messages and attended fourteen of the fifteen meetings.

We delivered our work product in time for our client's closing.

The last day of the project started at 4:00 a.m. for the working mother. When I arrived at 7:45 a.m., I was greeted by our Director of First Impressions. She told me our associate had been there since 4:00 a.m. and her baby was next to her in a playpen. The receptionist thought it was unreasonable that we required a young mother to meet such expectations. When I had left the night before, I was told the associate was returning early the next morning, but I had no idea she meant 4:00 a.m.--with baby in tow. Within the hour we moved the baby and playpen to the reception area. The baby and our Director of First Impressions got along splendidly. At 2:00 p.m. we delivered the report.

Mother and baby went home and spent the next business day and a half together, with pay and our blessings.

Things seemed impossible, but the new system worked and everything got done.

The two emergency projects were completed by the weekend. One of the teams included a tax associate, an audit associate and one of our support staff members. What a cross functional team--and it worked very well! The other project was completed by a shareholder who canceled an out of town trip to perform the work. I got home in time for dinner on both Thursday and Friday nights.

The newspaper article was published in Sunday's paper. The presidential search committee appointments were made public. The car battery problem was a loose connection. The city councilman wanted me to serve on a nominations committee, a relatively harmless assignment. I believe the two prospective clients will hire us.

The office actually seemed to enjoy my admission that for a few days I lost control of my own schedule.

In the meantime, I have restructured my agenda for the training course and it should be much more effective than it would have been had I taught the course as scheduled. This weekend, I will call my parents. Next week, I will try to sell a golf sponsorship or two.

Five years ago, the story would have been quite different.

I may have delegated several of my messages and less important meetings to "subordinates." Now, I believe if someone has called me, they probably want to talk to *me*, not to someone *else*.

The associate working on the project related to the sale of a client's business would not have considered bringing her baby to the office five years ago. Without her, I would have been unable to produce the computer-generated financial statements. As a result, we would have missed the client's deadline by at least four hours.

In the old days that would have been permissible, because clients were accustomed to waiting on accountants and attorneys. That is clearly not the case in today's environment.

The other two emergency projects may not have been completed five years ago. We would not have considered sending a support staff person into the field, and tax people were generally not considered for such assignments. Now, we search for appropriate skill sets instead of normal job descriptions.

Yes, there was dissatisfaction and some negatives to face. So what! Nobody's perfect.

As for dissatisfaction in the office, most of the underlying reasons provided to me by several sources were "on point"--even those that apparently contradicted each other.

After reflecting on these difficulties, I reminded myself of a statement I had made earlier. I told everyone in our office that implementation of the Atomic Model would be the most difficult change we had undertaken. I anticipated personal casualties. I believed these statements or I would not have made them. Why should reports of dissatisfaction have discouraged me?

I should have expected it.

So what have I learned? How much have I grown as a leader? What will I do next week?

I will return to the office with a heightened appreciation for the difficulties caused by change.

I need to resist the temptation to search for people who have not "climbed on board." Our traditional culture would have identified the resistance and dealt with it swiftly, an approach which worked well in a fear-driven environment.

However, we are not what we used to be. Reverting to our past habits would have disastrous results. Something else has become apparent to me--the importance of a 100 percent success rate in recruiting people to our firm who are well-suited to performing in our dynamic culture. In the traditional staid culture, a 33 percent recruiting success rate was expected and 50 percent would have earned the partner in charge of recruiting a special incentive award. Previously, if we missed on a few recruiting decisions, it did not matter. For the first two or three years on the job no one was expected to be happy. They were expected to keep their heads down. During this period the inexperienced staff did not participate in whatever few changes were occurring.

The week of my return from vacation reminded me of how much we are expecting of our people--especially the younger associates. Many of them have accepted responsibilities much sooner than the last generation of accountants did. The more experienced people must recognize this and support our younger leadership.

Next, I must acknowledge the difficulties resulting from change and the dissatisfaction which accompanies it. I must remind people of the "why" behind these changes.

At stake is the survival of our firm.

I need to remind everyone in the firm of our Aim:

- **To become the preferred business advisors for our clients;**
- **To work less and make more;**
- **To ensure our firm's long term viability.**

I need to remind our people that anything less than total commitment from every individual will slow our progress. I must clearly explain to everyone that change produces some nasty side effects and we should expect them rather than be discouraged by them. I must give encouragement to everyone, especially those at the center of our change efforts. I need to step up the communication effort by reinforcing the *positive* instead of becoming strangled by the *negative.* I need to ask our Noname Team the same questions Price Pritchett asks in his book, ***Resistance--Moving Beyond the Barriers to Change.***

> "Day in, and day out, what sort of example do you set? Are you personally a role model for adaptability? Do you lead others into change...or do you somehow lead them into resistance? Consider how many people take their cue from you. Ask yourself what kind of influence you carry. And when change hits, remember to move yourself first, so you don't get in the way of others."

Although I was initially discouraged upon return from vacation, I soon realized I had many reasons to be thankful. From now on, I begin each week with a renewed resolve to stay the course and continue the journey!

--Earl Maxwell

The Outside Help: Change, from a Consultant's Perspective

by Karl Krumm, Ph.D.

- ♦ What it takes ♦ Commitment to learning ♦ Ownership
- ♦ What to change ♦ It takes time ♦ Courage

Most change efforts fail to yield the benefits desired. Most organizations are not prepared to face the ups and downs of change, nor exhibit the persistence required to arrive at their destiny. The ML&R story captured on the preceding pages attests to the difficulties and the triumphs of such an effort. I have been fortunate to be part of this change effort. Since I have been an "outsider" of sorts, there are some things that I have noticed and learned.

What it takes.

When I first met the ML&R partners in my office, I was impressed by their sincerity and commitment to build an organization which was not only significantly different from most CPA firms, but from most organizations.

Earl Maxwell's motivation was twofold: *economic* and *philosophical.*

The economic motivation was clear. The firm was not prospering and in danger of closing its doors if something didn't change. This motivation of economic survival was not different from most organizations in desperate need of change in the increasingly competitive market place. The real difference was their intense desire to build an organization which treated its members, *all its members*, with a high degree of *trust* and *respect.*

They wanted to create an environment where "people could do things because they wanted to, not because they were afraid not to."

The second motivation was philosophical. This fundamental force driving change was born out of the partners' past experience with other firms, in which people were not trusted or valued. This philosophical motivation set ML&R apart from other organizations and has sustained its efforts to change in the face of many challenges. The desire to change was not just business, but personal. The force for change wasn't just economical, but a commitment to people and a pursuit of a larger dream of a healthy way of life beyond doing business.

I have come to believe that true change in an organization can only be accomplished when driven and guided by a set of *core values* that puts *people* and *relationships first.* The *economic benefits* are a by-product of this commitment. This was the competitive advantage for Maxwell Locke & Ritter and captured my interest in being part of their efforts.

Commitment to learning.

The people at ML&R are committed to learning. They don't just keep up with the trade and practice of accounting, but read and study all aspects of business and the human side of work. They are, and continue to be, hungry for new ideas and ways of thinking, organizing and serving their people. They read, listen to tapes, attend conferences and listen to their customers. They are willing to risk trying new approaches and tactics, but only if they are consistent with their core values. I have found them open to new ideas and alternative ways to manage, compensate and support their people. The willingness not only to be *open*, but to pursue *learning* sets them apart.

Ownership.

The change effort at ML&R was *theirs*. Although they have allowed me to be a part of their growth, they maintain ownership of the effort. Even though outside consultants can offer perspective and knowledge, successful change efforts are driven by those in the organization itself. There are many "change programs" and many consulting firms that are more than willing to set up and run an organizational development program. However, if the effort becomes owned by the consultant or is seen as an outside program, it is condemned to fail.

Earl has captured and described the role I have played quite accurately in the preceding chapters. Our meetings consisted of my offering ideas, posing a series of questions, and provoking thought. They discussed, argued, dialogued, and explored those offerings. It was between our periodic meetings that the real work was done by the people of ML&R who took these ideas and created applications and pilot projects to implement changes that fit their firm and their core values.

Throughout my work with ML&R, the change effort has always been theirs, not mine. They own it. A popular quote, "People don't resist change, only resist being changed" is true. Their success and sometimes failure to change rests with those that are living the ML&R story. Successful change happens only when the people involved have *ownership* of their own fate.

What to change.

Where do you start? In the beginning, ML&R made an important decision. Many organizations start by forming a change group to lead the effort. This team operates outside the existing management structure and attempts to implement changes in the formal organization.

ML&R chose a different path. *They radically changed the management structure itself.* They decided to form four teams which took over the major management functions: The Common Area Team, the Technology Team, the Marketing Team, and the Human Resources Team. Each team managed an important area of the organization. The result was to truly share ownership for the changes and to give everyone an opportunity in the governance of the firm. This early decision clearly was driven by their core values and helped reduce the resistance that many change efforts notoriously generate.

The direction and overall management of the organization was still held by the management group (Noname Team) but membership of this team was also expanded to include all levels of the organization, from different practice areas to part time workers.

The Noname Team has gradually allowed decisions to be made by more people and by the people directly affected by the change. They designed and altered the methods by which people were compensated, benefits received, and work performance reviewed. The risk of *letting go* of a tightly held management center has been a crucial aspect of ML&R's success in getting changes implemented.

This decentralization of power was supported by a willingness to share all appropriate information with everyone. Each quarter, I watched Earl "do the numbers," putting up all financial information of earnings and expenses, even his own! This willingness to provide the teams with important information was key in ML&R's ability to develop workable and successful changes in their business practices. *It also fostered trust.*

The changes continue to be driven by a system of management practices which has deemphasized a hierarchy and emphasized core values of openness, trust and belief in their people. The change effort became a new way of management that went beyond the usual tinkering with work processes and compensation plans in order to manipulate employees.

In order for change to prosper, an organization must change more than cosmetically. The choice to radically change the firm governance was the right place for ML&R to start.

It takes time.

Change takes a long time. In their first three years of meetings, the "tax" people sat on one side of the room and the "audit" people on the other. They continued to largely define themselves as a member of one faction or the other. **This has been one of the most consistent and frustrating barriers to changing their business practices.**

Even Earl's conducting a meeting with a box on his head, admonishing his associates to "think outside the box" did little to change this rigid membership structure. In the last year, we have spent a lot of effort attempting to shift people's mind-sets toward seeing themselves as providers of many services and skills.

Self-perceptions and perceptions of others are stumbling blocks to developing a responsive and integrated workforce of professionals who can be deployed where the work is needed and shift as the work demands change.

In recent months, with the development of the Atomic Model, *the shifts are beginning to take place.* Providing a model for people to see where they fit in a structure has helped.

It is clear that not everyone takes to change.

In an impressive presentation, Earl stated openly that he expected some of the ML&R people would not stay because of the changes. He not only gave permission for people to leave, but offered them his blessings and assistance in finding a better place for them to prosper.

Another interesting pathway of change has been the influx of new people into the firm. The "new kids" have never worked in the traditional organization. They do not have the same appreciation as the "old timers" for the history of changes that have already taken place at ML&R. However, who knows what innovations they may bring to the firm.

In order to promote change, one has to have the *urgency* to drive change and the *patience* to endure the length of time profound change requires. Altering the "mind set" or mental model is essential, and demands much effort early on.

Courage.

Change is hard and uncomfortable. The easy type of change is a transition in which one knows where one is starting and where one will finish. Moving from a manual to a computer-driven system has definable beginning and end points. However, transformational change, in which one knows something about the starting point but little of the destination, is much more difficult: the present reality is at least familiar, but the new reality is uncertain and ever changing.

The necessary ingredient for this type of change is *courage:*

- Courage to begin forsaking the known for the unknown;
- Courage to embark on a path and ask others to join you in leaving the familiar for a future you hope and believe will be better;
- Courage to continue when you are tired, or have lost the path, or when the path is much more unpopular than you anticipated.

A leader in organizational change must have this kind of courage. Earl is such a leader. He has been able to convince others to follow his direction based on his conviction and courage.

Courage is required to open oneself to challenge, debate and to be wrong. It takes courage to let go of power and trust one's associates to hold themselves accountable for results.

It also requires the "critical mass" of an organization to push and sustain change. I have seen others step up and lead for change in Earl's absence or because of their desire to make things better and different. This shared leadership takes place in the context of shared ownership for the outcome, open communication of vital information, and in alignment of shared core values.

I recently attended a stakeholders meeting of ML&R. I was once again moved by the level of excitement and honesty at that meeting. ***People talked! People dialogued!*** People shared their hopes and fears.

It's easy to come away with a renewed sense of excitement about the possibilities for the future. New dreams are being born. That's what transformational change is really about:

"People working together because they want to, not because they have to."

--Karl Krumm, Ph.D.

The First Ten Steps

1. The leading partner of the firm must be convinced of the new approach and absolutely committed to the conversion process.

2. The rest of the partners must commit to an appropriate level of support. A majority of the partners must be absolutely committed, while the minority must commit not to sabotage or undermine the changes ahead.

3. All partners must understand the leading partner will not tolerate any behavior that contradicts the new direction of the firm.

4. People will leave. Not everyone in your firm will be willing or able to make the fundamental changes that are necessary. On this issue, honesty, humility and compassion are more important than rigid employer-employee tradition.

5. Obtain outside assistance. We almost abandoned this new approach after two years of attempting it on our own.

6. Willingness to go to any lengths to change means just that. Do not attempt to piecemeal certain aspects of this approach. A slow death would be easier than the consequences of an haphazard attempt at this new approach.

7. Commit at least two or three years to the transformation process. Do not place the expectations bar too high. The change will take longer than you expect. Anyone expecting short-term tangible results will be disappointed and the firm will become discouraged.

8. Commit to a dedicated training program over a two to three year period. The fundamental concepts of this transformation appear deceptively simple. In reality, they contradict everything we have learned about organizational behavior and management during the twentieth century.

9. Learn the fundamentals. Row a little boat, before you attempt to sail. Then comes implementation. Do the easier things first--process teams, open communication, family friendly attitudes, and building a sense of community. The rest will follow as your organization wills.

10. Stay the course. Adopt Winston Churchill's favorite saying: "Never...never...never give up." Your firm will need this kind of determination as you approach this difficult journey.

Ten Mistakes to Avoid

1. Remember that "insanity is doing the same thing over and over again and expecting a different result." However, not all your people appreciate the nature of the changes occurring in the business world, or society in general. Many of them see little reason for fundamental change.

2. Do not assume that your people trust you, management, or the firm. Few people under fifty trust either authority figures or the institutions they represent. There is good reason for this mistrust.

3. Do not assume that all Xers are weird. Different, but not always weird.

4. Do not assume all of your people know how to effectively operate in teams, or in a "flattened" organization. Not everyone wants to be "empowered." More people are fans of Dilbert than cultural transformation.

5. Do not assume accountants think in terms of processes, or that they believe the concept of rework even remotely applies to them.

6. Do not move the postage meter without consulting the operator.

7. Do not assume communication will immediately improve as a result of your efforts. Also, your efforts will not increase the bottom line in the short term.

8. Do not underestimate the amount of time or energy involved in fundamentally changing your firm's business culture.

9. Do not forget "The Six Phases of a Project:"

    1. Enthusiasm
    2. Disillusionment
    3. Panic
    4. Search for the Guilty
    5. Punishment of the Innocent
    6. Praise and Honors for the Non-Participants

10. Do not forget that the long-term viability of your firm is at stake. The reality is you must fundamentally change, or die a slow death.

Acknowledgments

Many people, with support from The Almighty, contributed to this book. *My sincere thanks goes to all of you.*

Coleith Molstad worked closely with me in planning and organizing the contents of this book. Notes, prepared by her, contributed greatly to Chapters 2 and 6. Coleith wrote the initial version of Chapter 13. She has worked tirelessly to develop, introduce and implement the Atomic Model in our office.

The illustrations which give life to our words and deeds are by Wendy Winkler. The graphics presented in the book were created by Whitney Madere who, along with Coleith, has worked on the Atomic Model.

Karl Krumm, our independent consultant since 1993, shares with the reader his unique perspectives in the Outside Help chapter.

I am grateful to Sue Laurent for her letter welcoming new associates. That message is woven into this book.

Steve Best encouraged and inspired me throughout the process of writing the book.

Terry Matula assisted me in overcoming the technical challenges of becoming my own word processing specialist.

Jane Jones contributed her artistic talents to the cover design and general appearance of the book. She keeps me laughing and continually challenges me to "walk the talk."

Cynthia Wilson provided editing skills that were critical to converting my writing to something readable.

Mike Plake poured his body, mind and spirit into transforming the original manuscript into the book product you have read. We could not have achieved publication without Mike's experience and guidance.

Thank you to my fellow shareholders Tom Locke, Mark Ritter and Steven Knebel who have supported our reengineering efforts every step of the past six-and-one-half years.

Thank you to all my colleagues at Maxwell Locke & Ritter, p.c., past and present, who made possible the journey described and the stories told in this book. This book is about you.

Thank you to our clients and friends who made this journey possible. We appreciate the confidence and trust with which you have honored us.

On Thursday mornings for the past seven years, a group of people from all walks of life have met to invoke the name of the Almighty. Together, we learn, seek wisdom and support each other. These friends have influenced me, quietly and powerfully, to put into practice the important principles explored in this book.

Thank you to my wife, Anita, who has been a wonderful partner, friend, and advisor for the past twenty-three years. My two sons, Robby and Sam, have contributed in many ways. They have generally tolerated a Dad who is in too many places, too often, and drives them to see far more historical sites on family vacations than they really desire.

Finally, thank you to my parents who always encouraged their children to make the most of what we had. They instilled in us the core values that enabled us to become successful, each in our own right.

--*Earl Maxwell*

Centers of Influence

Many people shaped this book by shaping me:

Pages IX-XI of the preface depict Fourteen Points reprinted from *Out of the Crisis* by Dr. W. Edwards Deming by permission of MIT and The W. Edwards Deming Institute. Published by MIT, Center for Advanced Educational Services, Cambridge, MA 02139. Copyright 1986 by The W. Edwards Deming Institute.

The passages on pages 141 and 142 are from *The Employee Handbook for a Radically Changing World* by Price Pritchett, Ph.D. This is reprinted by permission of Pritchett & Associates, Inc., Copyright, 1994. More valuable advice from Mr. Pritchett was included on page 213, from *Resistance: Moving Beyond the Barriers to Change.* This is reprinted by permission of Pritchett & Associates, Inc., Copyright, 1996.

There have been many other guides on my journey--Peter Block and his pivotal work, *Stewardship: Choosing Service Over Self Interest*; Stephen Covey's *First Things First* and *Seven Habits of Highly Effective People*; Peter F. Drucker's *Managing the Future* and *Managing in a Time of Great Change*; Herb Kelleher and his incredible insight on total quality management; Zig Ziglar, his teachings, and his book, *See You at the Top*; Tom Peters and Robert H. Waterman, Jr., *In Search of Excellence*; Tom Peters, *Thriving on Chaos*; James C. Collins and Jerry L. Porras, *Built to Last*; Eliyahu M. Goldratt, *The Goal: A Process of Ongoing Improvement*; Gary Hamel and C. K. Prahalad, *Competing for the Future*; Lee Iacocca, *Iacocca* and *Talking Straight*; Spencer Johnson, *The Precious Present*; Jon R.

Katzenbach and Douglas K. Smith, *The Wisdom of Teams*; Patrick J. McKenna and Gerald A. Riskin, *Herding Cats*; Jacob Needleman, *Money and the Meaning of Life*; Peter Senge, *The Fifth Dimension: The Art and Practice of Learning Organization/Cassettes*; Ralph Stayer, *Flight of the Buffalo: Soaring to Excellence, Learning to Let Employees Lead.*

--Earl Maxwell